Journey of Awakening and Higher Consciousness

JANE KIM YU

Journey of Awakening and Higher Consciousness

Copyright © 2023 by Jane Kim Yu

Publisher: Absolute Author Publishing House

Editor: Dr. Melissa Caudle

Formatting: Sherri Marteney

Cover Design: Rebecacovers

Hardback ISBN: 978-1-64953-929-8

Paperback ISBN: 978-1-64953-911-3

eBook ISBN: 978-1-64953-912-0

Dedication

To all those on the journey.

You are already home.

Acknowledgments

I t has been my lifelong dream to write a book. Writing for me has been and is a true passion and lifelong love, the kind that burns in your soul and warms you completely all the days of your life and more. This love has held me, kept me, and inspires me still. For the longest time, I could get nothing out. Someone once told me you can't write a book until you've lived some. After all this time, I can say I have lived, and then it became time to birth this book. I didn't expect this to be the first book I wrote, but this subject has intrigued me equally and as much as my love for writing, if not more, so much more. Writing is a love. The Journey of Awakening is a love. The expression of our humanity is a love. It has been my lifelong dream to give my love.

This is an offering of love.

To my mother and father, who bore me and showed me love the best they can. To my sister Jamie, who is the most amazing person I know. Our family always holds the seeds for our highest and greatest growth. The seed that holds the keys to our destiny. The love, that is. The eternal love that is within us all.

To Wendy Butera: For sharing your wisdom, kindness, and love with me. I am grateful for meeting someone like you this day and every day. Thank you for being my guide, friend, and inspiration. I would never have survived without you.

To humanity: They say every person you meet plays a part in the story of your life, and it's true. We become the people we love because of those we meet and all that evokes within and, eventually, the natural transformation of one's soul as we do our inner work. We are all walking ourselves and each other home. There are no words to this gravity and majesty, for it is true in every way. To those I have met and to those I have not met, we are all connected. Thank you, and God Bless.

Mother Teresa, Gandhi, St Teresa Avila, St Therese of Lisieux. Each person inspires me like no other person can in life or history. Each person presents a part of my passion and a part of my soul. I deeply believe in love and the sacred nature of our life's journey. Reading and learning about these people helped me keep the faith and hold on to this love within and the love without as I walked my path, found my way, and continued with the passing of each loving day.

Thank you to God, the Divine, the Universe, the One who gives us life and breath. With all my heart, thank you. There are no words to express my undying gratitude for the gift of life I have been given—the opportunity to live, breathe, and come to be. The exquisite beauty life is and the exquisite beauty that we are. All I am left with, all I can say, all I can utter, is - thank you. Thank you with all that I am, and with all my love, my deepest love. I love you and thank you.

Contents

Preface

H ello there, and thank you for picking up my book. I have always been fascinated, obsessed, mesmerized, enchanted, and enamored with one thing and one thing alone for a very long time, what it all means: higher consciousness, enlightenment, or simply, what it means to live and be alive. Why do we use such big words for simple things? I suppose that's just how it is sometimes. We overcomplicate the most basic of all things. Things that are innate to who we are, the reason we live, and the air we breathe. Things like, Love.

Questions of this nature mattered deeply to me. They consumed me. They filled me. They lifted me. They also puzzled me. They challenged me. Yet, oddly, they pushed me because I wanted to know. Questions like, what does it mean to be a good person, to live a good life, and to live in peace? What is happiness, and can I achieve it, freedom of the soul, and more? Is enlightenment possible today and not just in old books from older people from a bygone time? Could it be? Could it be done now? And most of all, could I be it, do it, and have it? Could I dream it into existence, everything I wish for and more?

Out of all the things one can wish for, it wasn't the fairy tale, the daydream, the fantasy most people dream of and dream for. It was this. This was the most incredible dream I could conceive, and I wished for it with all my heart. It filled me so profoundly that it held me in eternal perpetuity until it came to be. That is the nature of destiny. It is the seed of the soul that desires to be until it simply is, and then the continual unfolding long after that.

Yet, it was also the greatest, the deepest, the most biting and excruciating pain in my life. We all endure pain, but this pain was a pain unlike any other that profoundly impacted my life in ways I can't even begin to describe. A pain with such sorrow and sadness. A pain with such loss and grief. A pain one walks and bares alone. Because of this and through various experiences in my life, this became the one question I wanted above all else. It became the one question I needed above all else. It simply became the one guiding question of my life.

And so, I devoted myself to this and this alone; I devoted myself to this path. I devoted myself to the path of peace the best I could. I devoted myself to love the best I could, even when I didn't know much of anything. In truth, who does when you're starting? But the greatest truth, even beyond that, is that we all start where we are, which is always the best place to be. All we need to do is wish wholeheartedly; everything is inevitable.

If you had or suffered the same questions. Came alive by the same questions. Had the same overwhelming, overriding, all-consuming desires. Had the dream that no one ever dared dream. The dream to come alive to the fullness of one's stature and one's name, one's true name, that is, one's sacred name. Yes. The name of love itself. Yes, that you are this love, this book is for you.

This is what I've learned.

You are the light of the world. The light of consciousness means more presence, awareness, insight, feeling, understanding, and compassion. Yes, simply more light.

Once you've tasted this, held this, smelled this, seen this, heard this, felt this, and experienced this to any discernible degree, you can never be the same again. Hence, life will never be the same again, for you are on the path that only a few dare and venture. You are on the path that all the greats of all time past all traversed. You are on the path, the great journey within, to discover the truth of who you are.

To honor our light is the most honorable and noble goal one can ever have in life. It is about facing all the love, accepting all the love, realizing you are the love, sinking into this love, and then the unleashing of your love. It is love manifest and love manifests in its highest form as you define it, refine it, and simply be it. Yes. You.

We may never meet in this life, but I know we walk the same journey. Forever the eager student, eyes wide open, heart wide open, soul wide open. You are rare indeed. It takes a rare individual to want more, be better, and go higher. It takes a rare individual to drop all the hate and lower energies behind. It takes a rare individual to finally face oneself. It takes a rare individual to finally accept all the love within and without. It takes a rare individual to finally live and come alive.

God Bless,

Jane

Journey of Awakening and Higher Consciousness

CHAPTER ONE

Journey Back to Your Heart

"Who looks outside, dreams; who looks inside, awakes."
— *Carl Gustav Jung*

L ove is the one thing humanity has been obsessed over. More than wars, catastrophes, and calamities. Beyond all this, this singular journey has captivated humanity since the dawn of time. From Plato, Aristotle, and Socrates to our current thought leaders of all and every kind, and not just philosophers but those of every faith and tradition, the poets, writers, activists, and artists. It has been the way of things and shall continue to be the way long after we are gone, for there is nothing greater than love.

We may come from different backgrounds, lives, and circumstances, but one thing remains and is the same. We share the same journey, the journey of awakening, the journey to return home to the heart. Yes.

Deeper than enlightenment.

Deeper than awakening.

Deeper than all of that.

When we live in our hearts, we automatically come to know what there is to know in every way and every level in such a way that meets our needs, fulfills our peace, and fulfills the seeds of our divine destiny. If we only keep the faith and choose to love the best we can. Then, it is all done before it has begun.

Many think enlightenment is foreign and impossible, let alone an unattainable concept, and isn't even the language funny? People coin it as a concept versus a reality. When the truth of the matter is when you live in your heart, it's already a reality. It's the only reality, that is. As we live our lives, so does our awareness and consciousness naturally grow toward this knowingness because that has been our focus and aim, to live by and through the heart. Nothing else feels as good or is as satisfying as so. So, eventually, it's where we all go. Simply back to the heart.

Throughout all time and space, many have called it enlightenment, satori, revelation, nirvana, insight, bodhi, and the list goes on and on.

Have you noticed there are so many names for the same thing?

There are so many names across all time, space, cultures, and races; it is endless.

But what it all boils down to is all the same.

It is, above all, humanity's journey, our shared journey, our universal journey.

The journey to awaken.

The journey to come alive.

The journey back home, to love itself.

To who you truly are.

And who are you? These are all names for the same thing. Love. When you open yourself up to the depth of love within, and thereby all that is and more. You open yourself up to the more, even beyond that, for there is no end to who you truly are or all that is. That is the glory and the grace we get to live in as we claim the truth of who we are. Simply the sheer beauty of who we are as it miraculously unfolds before our eyes because we allowed it to unfold within first.

Love is the way and the answer to everything one can ever name or dream. Then, within time, we eventually know the kind of exquisite grace that leads you into the prairie fields of peace. The place we all dream of. The place we all come from. The place we all already are.

When you have nothing in life, a person has absolutely nothing, or you've lost all that you can bear so it seems, regardless of whether this is true or not, you have love. With that is the potential to break through and break free from all the limitations that bind and rise above in due time, if not divine time, and unearth the bliss that is thine.

Deeper than any mindset hack, love is the highest, and the only force, for nothing else is real and exists. For there is nothing more powerful, nor potent, nor greater than love. It's not the mind that gets you there. It's the heart.

Then why do I feel so much pain? Why are things so hard?

I suppose that is the journey of our lives, coming to embrace the depth of who we are, the depth of love itself, the sheer breadth of all that is, as we live, and redefine it for ourselves, the joy and the very meaning of our lives by shedding all that is less than, all that is false, all that no longer serves and claim our love. Which is you and the divine as one.

When we step into the truth of who we are, we raise our awareness, consciousness, vibration, and internal level of understanding that goes beyond where mere words will reach but to and from a place that is. You begin to operate from natural intelligence. Yes, you. For that is your alignment for and to you, your flow.

This is not a flow you feel only when you feel good, when things are going right, or when you're on top of the world. This is a deeper flow that is, like all that is, just as you are, as you simply are. It's all the same as we come to claim our one true name. That name is the sacred name of love, dearest.

For some of us, we wish deep down this was true. We feel it somewhere profoundly in our core, and a part of us, the deeper part, says yes regardless of whatever our mind might say. For some of us, we know this to be accurate, and that is the journey of our lives to beautiful wholeness, to live in fullness and everlasting joy as we get to honor our joy and give it for the rest of our days.

It is this that is the journey of all mankind.

This has always been, is now, and forever shall be.

A return to love itself.

And lastly, let me say you are loved.

And you are love.

Yes.

Yes, you are.

No matter how small the voice is, not allowing that in our life is the source, the root of our pain. It expresses itself through our emotions, which are a good indicator of where we are. We must be willing to feel and sit with our feelings honestly and openly to see this and to honor it, whatever it may be. Then, slowly, we get clues and ideas on what to do next, which direction to head to next, or simply what seems best at this moment in time.

Life is not about being happy 24/7 per se. It's through the experience of our emotions, by the experience of our life, that shows us where we are within ourselves. Learning to process, feel, and release our emotions is fundamental to well-being. Remember, love is a flow. There is a flow to all life itself, and there is a flow to your life as well. So, we must honor this flow by learning to let go and release it into the very ethers of this world, to Heaven itself.

And if we don't do these two things, feel and release, it builds until there is a breaking point. One way or another, it reflects in our lives. The pain and the cost of not honoring our voice, the deeper voice within. After some time, similar patterns reveal themselves in our lives as we begin to go within or simply as we live, and eventually, one finally acts; for now, it becomes more painful to not. Then, at this point, you finally choose.

You choose you.

You choose to try.

You choose to act.

You choose to do.

You begin the path of love everlast.

For whenever anyone chooses themselves, that is the path of love itself.

For you are love true.

You are love, dearest.

You are love, dearest.

You are love.

CHAPTER TWO

The Story

"I am not bound to win, but I am bound to be true. I am not bound to succeed, but I am bound to live up to what light I have." — *Abraham Lincoln*

My Story

For as long as I can remember, I was only ever interested in one thing and one thing alone. If you picked up this book, you know what it is. I wanted to know, and I genuinely wanted to know what there was to know, all the things I didn't know; I wanted to reach enlightenment. Or deeper than that, more than that, I wanted to know peace. With peace, I also wanted to know fulfillment. I wanted to know what it meant to be a good person. I don't know why, but I just did. I wanted to know what it was to live and be alive. To come truly and wholly alive. I wanted to know what it meant to live a good life.

Have you ever had a burning desire? The kind that consumes you whole? Well, this was mine. It's as old as I can remember. On many occasions in high school, I remember sitting by myself on the stone slab in the courtyard, wondering what the meaning of life was or thinking how I wished there was a handbook to life so I could do this thing called life right. That was a genuine concern and meaningful curiosity if not a great fascination. It held my attention and my interest to no end.

I have no idea why that's what came to mind, and that's what I cared about, but it must have been strong enough that even in high school, that's what I'd like to think about in my alone time, between everything else when life slowed down, my mind slowed down, or when I slowed down.

You see, I was not the smartest, the brightest, or the most astute kid at all. Frankly, if I had to be honest, I couldn't think too deeply at that age. My level of awareness was relatively low awareness which has nothing to do with intelligence. I got into a specialized high school through an entrance exam. Still, intellect and consciousness are separate matters, as most of us have figured out by now.

At that age, I did not have the conscious ability to process anything outside of my immediate world and, even more so, whatever was in front of me. We all evolve at different rates and levels throughout our life. There is a timing to our life. There is no judgment to this. That's just our fingerprint, the blueprint we were given. Awareness and awakening to self and soul. It's a lifelong journey and process.

Much like the Meyers Briggs Type Indicator (MBTI), a personality typology test based on Carl Jung's theories, he aimed to prove that our seemingly random behavior is not so random and more based on our individual preferences on how we perceive the world. It is among the most popular personality tools in Fortune 500 companies worldwide.

It provides a framework for understanding individual differences, drives, and value systems. It promotes greater understanding, self-awareness, community, and communication. For now, our differences are a source of strength and understanding for what they are, simply a different way of viewing the world versus labeling anyone terrible or wrong.

Four main categories sort you into one of sixteen personality types.

Introvert and Extrovert - Do you focus your energy on the outer world, or do you focus your energy on the inner world?

Sensing and Intuition - Do you focus on what's real and your five senses, or do you focus on associations and the possibilities of what could be?

Thinking and Feeling - Do you prefer to make decisions based on logic, or do you weigh human motives and values into it?

Judging and Perceiving - Do you prefer making orderly decisions and closure or being open to new ideas and spontaneity?

Understanding the various types gives us insight into our everyday lives, how we live our lives, and how each variation offers a whole new level and way of looking at the world.

On top of that, we all have our learning styles too. There are many variations of learning modalities, but these are the three basic types: Kinesthetic, Visual, and Auditory.

If you are a kinesthetic learner, you learn best by doing and taking hands-on action. Kinesthetic learners often struggle with learning the traditional way of sitting in a lecture. They must be actively involved to learn the material.

If you are a visual learner, you learn best by seeing graphs, pictures, and charts. They read body language well and have a keen eye for aesthetics like decorating or design.

If you are an auditory learner, you learn best by hearing and having notes read back aloud. Auditory learners ask lots of questions and discuss what they hear immediately. So, even the way we take in information is different.

Aside from MBTI, there are so many personality tests that reveal things we didn't see about ourselves from a different angle: our strengths and growth areas. Simply put, there are endless possibilities for the fingerprint of our being. Each is unique in its own right.

Often, instead of accepting and appreciating who we are, we criticize ourselves or others for not being like us or others when, in reality, each perspective has a valuable gift and insight that they bring. The mind tells us we're not good enough and should be more like this person or that person. In reality, we are simply all different and dazzling colored flowers in the beautiful garden of all heaven and earth.

How each style and mode and way of being serves. It serves not only you but the greater whole, too, how each perspective and person matters. How every person's unique way of being, especially, matters! To embrace what makes us unique and different is the gift and insight you offer and bring - if you only let it grow and embrace who you are.

And much like any person, we need time to grow. Grow into the truth of who we are as we claim it by working through our pain, releasing and accepting what is, and accepting who you are. Thereby, through acceptance, there is a complete rejuvenation of the truth of who we are little by little, bit by bit until you are. Learning to accept ourselves is a lifelong journey. With that comes the power to be. Be free. Be happy. Be you. Unconditionally. That is the purest freedom and our birthright when the heart and soul are free.

That would be my journey going forward as I would learn that. I don't want to say the hard way, but I suppose it was the way it was meant to be. Because, yes, some things are meant to be. Our lives are in divine order, beyond our knowing and comprehension. I wouldn't understand the very nature and truth of this until later in life. I can say this now, at this stage and age of my life. This is a fundamental truth of all life if not a law. All is in divine time and divine order, which is divine law. So, what is the journey of awakening, consciousness, higher consciousness, and love itself?

So, I bet by now you are wondering who this person is who is talking about all this. Yes, it's a good question, and I would also be wondering the same thing. I am no one—just someone who earnestly desires to grow and understand. I had an insatiable desire. An overruling desire. An unquenchable desire. It was, and forever shall be, my life's greatest joy and fascination. When anyone honestly asks these questions on the nature of who we are, the only answer, conclusion, anything, everything, there is but one, and that is - Love.

As I mentioned earlier, we all grow and evolve at different rates. Well, I was slower than most. My level of awareness was limited to quite an extent for an extended period, much like any child growing up. We all have our time for things and divine time at that. How all things happen for a reason and a purpose beyond our knowing or comprehension at the time, but all serve a higher goal if we let it.

So, a little about me.

I was sick for most of my life. I was severely allergic to the sun to such an extent every summer for at least ten years; the summer sun would be so intense for my skin that it would inflate and harden my face, neck, arms, and body parts. When it hardened, it would puff up like dragon scales and dry out so much that if a drop of water splashed, I would feel visceral pain like pin needles with each drop of water.

So, how did you take a shower? I couldn't. It was so painful I could not take a shower. My mother had to bathe me gently, and it stung every time, a thousand needles at once without fail every evening to no avail.

My face would bloat, scale, and harden to the point I could not move, and any movement would hurt. So, I drank water or soup out of a straw every 3-4 months out of the year for 10+ years because I couldn't physically do anything else. So naturally, I lost and gained a dramatic amount of weight every year with the summer sun.

I looked like any of those pictures in those medical textbooks—an extreme deformity. I was one of those. One day, you are an ordinary kid with regular issues; the next, your entire life changes, and you're a different kid with different issues.

I never asked why. I never asked why this happened, why it was happening, or why it was me. When you are a child, you don't ask why. You understand and accept that it is. Throughout the pain and the many long days, I accepted. Yes. I didn't like it, but I accepted. I didn't know any better.

Let alone, what else was I going to do? And so, I spent a quarter of every year in bed for a long time, just looking at the ceiling and the window if there was one.

My body was transformed every summer like the strange case of Dr. Jekyll and Mr. Hyde, and I felt like the elephant man in every way. Yet, for me, it wasn't a feeling or a story; it was true, and it was my story. If you read the book, it's about a man with a horrible disfigurement, and that was my reality. When your face bloats with scales covering your entire face and body parts to the point you can't move as well, there is not much you can do. I had to cover all the mirrors in the house because I couldn't manage to look at myself. It pained me, and I winced whenever I came near any reflective surface, for I was indeed a monster. This became my daily ritual.

This is how I learned to look down and not look anyone in the eyes. In fear of what I might see in the mirror or another person's eyes, the judgment, the sadness, the disgust. Or the truth that I so profoundly feared, that yes, I am genuinely unworthy, unredeemable, and unlovable. More profound than just ugly, but simply unlovable. That how I felt about myself, and what I saw in the mirror was what I am, which was unbearable.

It all started one day when I went to Six Flags with a church group in the summer. I learned I couldn't go out like the other kids because I was not like the other kids. Within 15 minutes of arriving in the morning, I passed out immediately and fell to the ground. The next time I opened my eyes, it was already late afternoon, and I was sitting on the Greyhound bus that took us here with a white handkerchief over my face. I felt something slowly oozing from my face and neck, which hurt to move. So, I just lay there, slightly reclined, and sat still.

I didn't know what was going on. All I knew was I felt pain, I could not move, and all the kids were getting on the bus after a long day watching me laying back in the seat in pain, all whispering what was wrong with her, what's up with her face, she looks like Godzilla. I didn't mind all the comments, mostly because I was half dazed and tired, but I was looking forward to going home and being with my mother.

From that moment on, that was the year that began it all. We went to the pediatrician and hospital, and no one knew what it was. Who has a sun allergy? Let alone with this level of reaction? I did. I remember the first year it was so bad; they took me to the hospital, and whatever they did was so painful I started screaming and writhing on the table. Several people had to hold me down. That is my memory of hospitals-the pain.

Being constantly sick did a number on my being. I don't know if I ever had self-esteem, self-worth, or self-anything as a kid. Still, as one can imagine, this yearly crippling deformation experience shred any last part of any clue I could have had. It took from me, me and gave me a new reality.

Fast forward a few years, and one night in particular, as I lay in bed looking at the same white ceiling, my familiar friend, I began to wonder if I would die and what death was. I began to cry because I did not want to die. I wanted to live. In that moment came the most genuine desire; my first desire was born. I wanted to live and understand what living and being alive meant. I asked God, whoever he was, I asked him as tears rolled down my face, lying down and writhing in pain, alone and by myself.

Dear God,

Please, oh please, give me one more day, day by day. I want to know what it means to live and come alive, and I promise I will use each day to do just that. I want to live! Please, just one more day, day by day, and I will.

Amen.

Was it a prayer, a calling, or all of these things? I cried my eyes out, and my entire pillow was soaked.

When you are physically disfigured and crippled, you begin to realize the value of health and, more profound than that, the value of living and being alive. The desire is there even if we don't know what that is, and we all have and share that desire. To be born and birthed anew.

Even kids. We have an accepting heart until the realization hits, and boy, did it hit. The finality of death and wrapping your head around that was a doozy. I turned old enough to realize this might be it and what that means.

So, I prayed. I prayed, again, and I prayed once more.

Then, I wished upon a star. With all my heart, I wished upon a star like in all the fairytales.

Father.

Please, take this pain away. I don't want to die when I haven't even lived yet. I want to live and know what it means to be alive. I will do everything I can to do just that! I promise. I promise with all my heart. I promise.

Amen.

I spent many nights with that singular prayer between everyday life's mental, emotional, and physical pain.

So, long story short, it did not go away. It lightened and lessened to a minimal degree with each passing year. Still, over decades, it's much better and manageable now. That was my first genuine prayer, desire, or wish. To live. I didn't want what other girls or kids wanted. I didn't care about a lot of things. I still don't. This shaped the direction I was going to go. Looking back now, I realize this was the beginning of my story (even before what happened next which radically changed it all.)

Fast forward many years later, I was walking on the university campus, and it was a beautiful, glorious day. The kind where the sun is shining, the clouds are puffy and nice, the gentle breeze caressing your skin now and then, the trees rustling in the wind as the leaves dance ever so gracefully. Not many people enjoy or even notice the leaves dance, but that's the sort of thing I always found so beautiful. When nature glistens and shimmers before your eyes and your heart.

As I was walking, delighting in the day, all of a sudden, everything began to slow down ever so softly. I felt a deep, loud, thunderous crack in my brain as if the ground beneath the feet of my being was giving way like an earthquake, as if a dusty, long-forgotten chasm had finally been revealed and opened within me. I felt a rush of energy and the great winds flowing through me, pouring into and from me, in my mind, heart, body, and very being.

I felt a surge of such light. I slowly stopped walking and stood still. I stood as still as possible, taking every morsel of emotion, energy, and light. It was so beautiful; I had to stop and stay still to feel it all because it was that good, exquisite, awe-inspiring, and all-encompassing. Simply awe-inducing. It was the most profound experience of my life. I don't know how long I stood there as all the students walked to and from class. It could have been minutes, or it could have been a few hours. I believe it was for quite some time because I only got home in the afternoon.

And so, I stood underneath the campus trees near St. Albert's Hall and took it all in. The beauty of the world, the beauty of humanity, the beauty of all that is. The beauty of everything, every last bit, and every last drop. I was consumed, enveloped, and taken. There was so much beauty. Such beauty goes beyond words that even such elegant words will never be able to convey, capture, or dream. No. True beauty is timeless, and words are mere trinkets. That's saying a lot because I love words. This is true.

The leaves didn't just sway and dance; they glowed now. They glowed with such a glow it took my breath away. All life glowed with such brilliant hues; it was unmistakable and undeniable, simply indescribable. Love was pouring from my eyes, love was pouring from the world, love was pouring from every face and facet. That was after the fact. In that exact moment when everything stood still. I only saw one thing—the light. The brilliant, warm, incandescent light opened my essence and swept me off my feet.

A surge of warm energy blew through me as if I were a mountain pass being brought to life at that very moment as all the debris fell away. Debris, I didn't even know I had in all the little pockets and crevices of our being; it all dissolved and disappeared. It no longer existed. This left an even greater opening within me as more light entered, illuminated every part, and consumed me entirely.

It was a true panacea, healing and revealing. There was nowhere to hide or go, nor was there any desire to do so. There was one desire: to feel it deeply, see it all through, revel in the bliss, and face it all, no matter what happens. It was a learning, unlearning, renewal, and revival. A true rejuvenation of soul and spirit. An unearthing of who we are. It is difficult to describe, but the truth is that if we genuinely get grounded, we all know what there is to know. For that lies deep within our hearts. Our innate inner wisdom. Our self and our soul. Wherever our faith may lie, we all have a heart. Our heart connects us to all that is and more, above and below, within and without, and in every way possible.

It's time to wake up now, dear. It's time to remember who you are dear. It's time to begin, dear. That was the feeling I felt. It was time.

After that profound moment, I lost all ability to think or process anything mentally, leading to another profound experience. I felt an earthquake cracking open the deepest chasms of my mind, heart, and soul. I felt it all, and I let go. It's like my mind opened, released, and turned off.

What happens when the thinking aspect of you calms down, comes to a slow standstill, and then stops completely? All you are left with is feeling. The land of milk and honey, as they say. The land of blissful, unadulterated, pure, raw feeling. The truth of who you are at your core. That yes, you are in love, and you are love, true. That love is the only reality, the only thing that is real, and the only thing that exists.

Yet beyond even that which sounds incredible, something also just turned on. The proverbial light switch had been turned on within my being. The experience of which was like night and day. This was my first experience with consciousness and my consciousness.

I knew silence, stillness, and complete and total peace for the first time.

I was. There was no wanting, no wishing, no willing. There was simply and only being. From being was the genuine appreciation of life and the beauty, miracles, majesty, and your life at that—the sheer experience of life and the honor of being alive. There were no more questions. There was one joy: to give love and receive love, simply to love. Not only was that the highest goal, but it was the only goal. The idea of being was no longer a mere idea but a factual matter and function of our visceral reality. We all are. We begin to see the truth when we get out of our way and learn to tame our minds. It's as natural as breathing, and it was that natural to me.

That was the moment my entire life changed.

Along with the experience of my mystery childhood sickness, my path was solidified. I needed to know what I needed to know.

All my wishes, yearnings, and prayers had been answered. However, this opened the door to even greater wishing, yearning, and even more feverous heartfelt prayers.

I needed to know what this was. What happened, and what was going on? What is this amazing feeling, this amazing experience, this amazing reality? Not so much. "Why is everything so beautiful?" As if one was questioning and puzzled but more so, "Oh my God, everything is so beautiful!" as a sheer statement of fact and wonderment.

It was the most exquisite peace I had ever felt or known. It shook me to my core because it opened my core. It was like the dusty covers of my heart and soul had been opened, yet a warm blanket had also been placed around me. Lastly, there is no blanket. Love is love, and love is universal, and there is no separation between you and love, you and the world, you and all that is. You from you.

This was the day I fell in love for the first time. It is the moment everyone waits for and wishes for in a partner, and it happened to me instead. It was powerful beyond measure. It was magical beyond measure. It was a treasure beyond treasure. Even the writing of this does not compare. Like any true love story, it has to be lived, experienced, and savored. Secondhand accounts or reading of it only does so much.

The memory of this event has faded over time. Not right away, of course. How could it? It was burned into my being. Something like this stays with you forever in many ways. Love always does.

It served as a guiding light throughout my journey of discovery, and the subtle effects of which still do. Whenever I forgot or whenever I struggled, the sheer memory and energy of this event alone lovingly kept me, held me, and reminded me of the truth of what is, of the bountiful love, the love that is at hand, the love that is, as we are! The reality goes beyond what we see but is much more profound. It is this we call eternity, for love is eternal.

And I, too, forget from time to time, but we are all human, are we not?

We are.

And how wonderful we are all in this thing called life together. For however long we have, what a gift and a blessing. We each carry with us and share the love we know and the love we are, which only grows deeper as we grow, too. That is how powerful we are and how powerful one true memory, act, emotion, and experience of love are. It simply illuminates our way and our lives. It acts as a beacon, a guiding light, a true north star. You don't need to see in the dark; all you have to do is hold onto the light, and the rest will figure itself out. It always does.

And so, back to our story.

Something profound happens when your mind stops fighting you, or when you stop fighting your mind, or in my case, the mind stops altogether. You are. In every way you are, you are fully present in what is.

If you are wondering what is "what is," that is you, the world, and all life itself. For you are life, and life and you are one. The beauty of this world is the beauty of you, and vice versa.

You lose, quiet, ease, or release all the mental and emotional baggage that you both did and did not know you had. When it all leaves, there is no separation, not anymore. For separation was from the mind and not the heart. All you're left with is you. All you're left with is everything and nothing at the same time. All you're left with is the beauty of what is—no more monkey mind, as the Buddhists say. No more chitter chatter or undue influence of any kind. Just pure being. The good old-fashioned kind. The kind everyone is looking for. If they only looked within.

And somehow, I now had not just the confidence, but also a deeper inner confidence based on the overflowing wellspring of joy I felt within my very being versus anything external as so many of us do and misguidedly place our faith.

It was the joy of being and the love for life and living. A proper reverence and appreciation for life's beauty, wonder, and grace. The love pouring from my soul, the souls of all those around me, and the soul of the world. All of it. The kind of love that radiates like the sun, glowing and flowing by and through your heart. There is no intellectualizing anything. You know. You know what you know, and you know it. Life is always that simple. Love is always that simple. All the good things in life are always this simple.

They say with love, you have endless enthusiasm for the task at hand. It's true. You naturally become resilient. That is an innumerable grace of love, one of many if we allow it, which means boundless, endless, never-ending joy!

To have all the shackles that bind come readily off and experience the joy called life, the joy called you, the joy called love, and to understand it's all the same. This was a freedom unlike any other. I was finally at peace. I was free. Free to be. Free to be me. Free to let my soul run wild and free, and I did.

With that, I knew my role in this life was to be love and happy. That was it. Whatever that may mean, and whatever that may be, it was about simply being me and letting my spirit fly free. It's not my role, but everyone's role. That is our purpose, the purpose of this life. Let alone, it's the only way to be happy and fulfilled and live by simply being ourselves, our true selves, ourselves unleashed. This was a deeper knowledge than intellectual semantics; this knowing ran down to my core, where I understood it on a visceral, guttural, if not biological, level. In that moment, my heart said yes, and I devoted myself and decided to do just so.

To give and give "this." Whatever "this" was, I wanted to give it.

I was going to give it.

I had no idea what that meant or what it would mean for me, but I knew I really would. Not because I had to, but because it is the only inevitable choice for anyone when you're there. For love must do what love does. Love must love, give, and honor one's heart and joy. Sharing is caring, after all, and love wants to have fun!

Some people experience this if they do, for a brief moment. That moment when time stands still, and you experience a radical heart opening, heart surrendering, heart revealing a true presence of a kind, through a traumatic event like a near-death experience of any sort, or an awakening to any degree, or even giving birth and looking into your baby's eyes for the first time. Whatever it may be, for the most part, it's usually a few moments that somehow feel longer than it is. Yet, it's all anyone ever needs. It's that powerful, potent, and raw that it brings a person back to life. That is the power of complete and pure presence. I lived in this moment for six solid months without break or interruption. To understand, know, and breathe bliss with every part of my being.

It was bliss.

It goes beyond what any storybook can capture. The entertainment business is built on capturing magic, but no one can quite capture this. Reality is always far better than fiction. The beauty of this is that incomprehensible, that indescribable, that ineffable, one cannot even begin to express, but feel, feel so deeply, in that act alone, you remember and reap the benefits because the energy of love and the allowing of this energy into your being is a true remembrance and healing, for it is you in every way at your core.

During this extraordinary time, the few questions that slowly arose within me were answered immediately, and should another question arise within me, another answer would arise again until I got to the depth of all the questions one may have. To go to the root itself from which all life comes. If you're wondering what that answer was. Yes, it was love, and that was peace. Peacefully profound and profoundly peaceful. To have no more questions, to know peace, and to simply breathe and be.

So, long story short, after six months, I began to lose it all, the state of grace that had so captivated, enchanted, and enamored my being for the entire summer as I was now entering the fall clinical years for my doctorate in school which was already hard enough but with this, it became one of the most complex and challenging times in and of my life.

We all endure challenging moments in life. So many to name and so many to count, it seems. However, the pain of the loss of Heaven itself, of bliss beyond bliss, of the purest love you've ever known, I'm not sure there is a pain quite like that one. Especially when you're a kid, and you have no idea what's going on except having this overwhelming, indescribable, palpable love burning within and without. With the experience of exquisite beauty came the experience of exquisite pain.

I could no longer unsee all I learned, felt, and lived through. I could no longer unsee me, the real me. I could no longer unsee many things. All the mental baggage I did and did not know I had came rushing back. Now, I had to face it, one by one, on top of clinical studies.

On top of that, there has been no understanding from anyone for a long time. I was going to face the world alone for a long time. That was my path.

When in life does something like this happen? I even began to question my sanity. I talked to many professionals and people with many doctorates and degrees, from the clergy to the scientists. Still, no one, not one person, had the language or a basis of understanding for this. This has nothing to do with your mind but entirely with the level of one's heart. That is a sacred, personal, ongoing journey for us all. So, there's nothing to do except to understand.

In your twenties, you only want to meet friends, have fun, and laugh. You have some unconscious behavior you're working through, if you're aware, but you want to have fun. Let alone when you've found the greatest love of all that burns in your being, and what does love want to do when it's found love? Love wants to give and share and play as any person does. I tried, but most people in their twenties don't care for such things or don't have the mental and emotional capacity to understand yet. I found no understanding or interest in the matter until much later in life.

To have experienced the most miraculous thing a person can ever see and face, and have it all go away, and then to have not a single soul know or even care to discuss matters of the depth of who we are, the depth of love itself, the depth and breadth and beauty of life. Or even to be present in what is, which is also a lot. This went far beyond personal development, psychology, philosophy, or anything the mind can construct or conceive, for it was all about the heart and that pained me to no end.

I was very depressed and sad for quite some time, going back and forth, struggling with this new reality versus the current state of things, the current state of me. How can I justify and rectify this new way of being? And in my heart, I knew this to be true and not only the ideal way of life and living but the only way to live and be. To be this free and happy and in sheer ecstasy and glee.

That began my journey to understand what happened, what I experienced, and what I discovered, to discover me.

And to discover yourself is to discover humanity. To discover humanity is to discover yourself. It's the same.

As are all our stories, the very reason we are alive is for this singular purpose alone. To discover and rediscover the depth of who we are, align with it, and be it, and then to give our love, whatever that may be. That is the purest fun, the purest joy, the purest ecstasy there is, that fills and fulfills our heart and soul to no end and no measure, with complete and utter satisfaction and satiation.

One of the many greatest gifts in life.

Should we honor our calling?

Should we honor our hearts?

Should we honor our being?

To know – Ecstasy. Bliss. Beauty.

To know – Love that burns true.

To know – You.

It's always about you.

So, this book is not about me.

It's a story about you and your journey.

So, let's get on with it.

Your Story

This is all about you, not me. Yet are we so different? We may or may not know each other, but we breathe, live, and feel. The same emotions of hurt, sorrow, pain, joy, happiness, and contentment when it comes. That is the human journey, the journey of all our beings as we explore this world and, more importantly, explore ourselves and the depths of ourselves as we live and breathe. That is the grace and the beauty of what it means to be human and alive.

So, let's talk about us.

You and me and all humanity. People.

No matter how different we are, we are all the same. At our core, at our heart, from the very start, we were babies born anew to this world, fresh babes with a clean slate. As we lived and grew, we took on the beliefs of our immediate family and our environment, as they were given to us or placed upon us, and then the beliefs we willingly took on for ourselves.

As we grew, we learned to shed old false beliefs and patterns bit by bit to adopt anew. Or was it simply a release and a renewal to the deeper truths of who we truly are? That feeling we all feel but can't quite grasp at times, and our sincere wish that it was true, that it could and would be true, to just be. That being aspect, in quality, in place, in feeling, in tone, in aliveness, in peace, in passion, in purity. That happy place we all have deep down. Can it be?

Yes, it is meant to be.

One thing is universal throughout this journey: regardless of our varied life circumstances and conditions, there comes a time, if not many times, when we get a pull within our heart to listen to the heart. Yes. It is literally that simple.

Listening to the heart, the heart call, the heart tug, the heart pull are the same thing. One may not need to have the experience I did, but regardless of the situation, a heart pull is a heart pull. That's what it boils down to. The honoring of the higher voice within. The deeper voice. The sacred voice. Simply your voice. The voice of your heart and soul.

Yet who will listen? That's what they mean when they say many are called, but few are chosen. For who will choose love itself? Who will choose the loving way? Who will choose to listen to their heart, whatever it may mean, regardless of cost? Only the brave listen to the heart, the strong listen to their heart, and the courageous listen to the heart. Simply those true of heart. Simply those filled with love. Simply those aligned with who they are and strive to do so.

And ultimately, is there a more significant cost than the price of one's soul? For that's what it is, whenever we deny self, dishonor self, and do not nurture and nourish self. Alignment sounds like a big word, but it just means listening to your heart. Everyone overcomplicates everything. Let's make it simple.

But wait!

Then you say, my heart says a lot of things! I have so many thoughts and feelings. I don't know sometimes! Yes, of course, but beyond thinking, there is an underlying presence, a depth if you will, that always heals, heals every place and every part of our being until we are free. A deeper place, space, and grace lives within us all. That is the space of your heart. Yes. Your heart space.

This place will never guide you wrong. It will always guide you right. No matter what it is. No matter who we are. No matter the level of awareness we may possess. No matter the level of consciousness we may be at present. Regardless of our intelligence level also. It doesn't matter. There is a place and a space deeper than all the things that bind, and that is your heart. Your heart speaks in gut feelings, in between your thoughts, in between the depth of feeling, in between the silence and stillness; it's your knowingness.

By honoring how you feel, not the chaotic mind, but the softness of one's kind, which is the grace that guides when we can lay down our arms, lay down all our pain, lay down everything we hold dear, and choose the loving way. Then all that is dear is given and shown to us, for that is the way of things. Once we open and surrender, we are given eternity's wonder and splendor.

When we live in our hearts, it solves many problems, and the problems in our lives become opportunities that propel us into our greatest destiny. Destiny is not a farfetched concept nor an intangible, impossible, improbable ask. Destiny is divine decree, for are you not divine and a part of the divine? Yes. Destiny is meant to be, for it is your soul's calling. Soul callings can never be denied and always come in time. It takes honoring our heart for it to truly shine.

It helps you realize and understand who we are, the more of who we are, the beauty of who we are in such profound ways, simply because your heart is open and open to the awareness of what it is learning at this time. Deeper than the lesson in each opportunity, event, or challenge, but the higher lessons as well, which are, in fact, beyond priceless but timeless. Everything in this life always roots and stems and takes you back home, home into your heart, Heaven, and the sweet evergreen garden that's forever in flow, and that is the truest journey. The greatest journey. The journey of all mankind.

Simply, your journey of the sublime, dearest.

Once we lock into that, all pain fades, for a higher knowingness comes into play and a deeper understanding that says it's all okay. Finally, every part of you agrees, accepts this decision, and releases and relaxes into yourself. The truth of who you are in greater measure. In return for this faith, or return for your surrender, or in return for your love, comes the grace to be in a greater measure as well.

Sometimes, people say choosing the loving way is too complicated and costs me too much. It's not worth it, or I'm scared. Well. It's okay. Sometimes, we grow up in environments that are not conducive to loving thoughts or nurturing our well-being.

When we are not shown, taught, or don't see it in our home environment, we can't model it in ourselves and our lives because we don't have a baseline understanding. The energy of whatever we lack, the denial of love in one form or another, builds up over time and eventually expresses itself throughout various manifestations in our lives. All representations of the various areas of growth our soul is calling for. Sometimes, the learning is mild and minimal, and sometimes, the learning is bitingly complex.

It's okay. It is. Everything has a higher purpose and serves your greater good and the whole. No matter how we were raised or our life circumstances, deep down, we all feel when it comes down to it. We feel beyond the surface feelings but the depth of feeling. There is that part of us that is like all that is. That part where you know the answers. That part where you know what the right thing would be to do. That part where you know what the loving response or action is. That part where you know this is what you want to do, no matter how scary. Or even if none of these apply to you at the time, the fact you allow feeling means you are open to the whispers of your heart, which is a miracle and all anyone ever needs and can ever do.

God bless all who walk upon this journey of inner healing, self-discovery, and more. That is the path: a multi-fold path. There is no one path. Simply by living, it is all inevitable, and that is the true, sheer, and utter grace of what is. Our simple desire for peace to get out of pain or the desire for more is the spark that also triggers the journey. Once you start, you can never go back. Once you've tasted that morsel of goodness, the goodness and the truth of who you are, that timeless quality, your entire life changes. That's a rabbit hole you can never unsee. Nor would you ever wish it.

That you would choose this. This life and this journey just as you are, over a thousand other lifetimes, because the learning from this life experience is so invaluable, delicious, delectable, and simply so rich you want to savor every morsel, for now you know each immaculate bite holds so much goodness to unpack. The kind of goodness that can illuminate a life for lifetimes to come and does. For it illuminates the entire world for all time to come. Yes, it is done.

What is that saying? Once you pop, you can't stop! Just like Pringles! Yes. Once you're being pops into higher consciousness, aka the depth of your heart, you can never return. Sure, we may swing back and forth here and there. The only way one finds peace in life, the only way one finds joy in life, and the only way one finds any fulfillment in life is by living by and through the heart. It is a true return to love and unconditional love.

That is the destiny of all mankind.

That is the path of illumination.

That is the only path any of us are actually on.

Yes.

And in truth, the most profound truth is that we all walk this path. We may or may not label it spiritual. Labels are irrelevant, and labels get us stuck. It is learning to accept, make peace, and love ourselves unconditionally. That's the most profound thing there is. That is core to who we are. That is the path. That is the way of love.

No matter what we do, what job we may have, or where we are placed in the world, every upset and experience takes us back home to who we are if we let it. In this way, it is deeper than a spiritual journey, but honestly, the universal journey of the deeper reality of all that truly is, should we choose it and allow it. To choose love itself. The loving way. The loving choice.

Which means choosing you.

What does it mean to choose you?

Honoring you.

Honoring your voice.

Honoring your love.

Honoring who you are.

In every way that you are.

That is what it means to choose you.

You will allow yourself to be yourself and release yourself into this world as you are. Love incarnate. The direction of your joy is up to you; a delicious choice as you choose it from your heart and soul. That is the sheer and utter beauty of life. The freedom to be and choose our reality, ecstasy, and immortality. By the honoring of our love and the giving of our love. The releasing of our love.

For with love, anything born with and from love lives on and lives long after we are gone. For the true nature, energy, depth, and breadth of love is so deep, all Heaven and Earth reaps till the ends of time itself.

This is how profound you are, dearest.

Have faith, go forward in faith, go forward in grace, go forward in love, and know you are divine, and your life is divine, and you walk with the divine. This, I can say for sure and know to be true.

How did David find the strength and courage to face Goliath against unspeakable and hopeless odds? How did Gandhi find the strength and the courage while still maintaining irresolute joy, service, and unwavering determination in his heart while facing an entire regime? How did Mother Teresa not tire from serving the endless sea of all humanity throughout her life, as written in her diaries? Yes.

How did anyone ever find the strength and courage to face their deepest demons, trials, or joys, within or without? How did anyone ever commit to their path regardless of all costs? It took the grace of faith as they allowed it into their heart and acted from their higher knowingness for their cause, the cause that lit their soul on fire. Faith is the bridge between dreams and reality. We are always the allower and the finisher of our faith. With that, there is always divine grace.

That is it.

With a clear purpose burning in their soul, there is only one way to go. When we feel it burning in our being, there can be no other way but so.

How often do we feel that burning within us all? It may come in different shapes and forms, but we all feel it. It may be as simple as a heart pang. When we hear our inner voice say, hey, we should be nicer here or choose to be considerate and care. In that split second, we decide. In that choice, that moment of decision, in that micro decision that went beyond thought but down to feeling, we choose our fate and destiny. This is how it builds from beyond the level of thought.

It's not about the big moments. It's about all the small moments. It's deeper than the small moments. It's about all the moments no one ever sees or knows. All the moments you feel within and choose within yourself. It goes that deep. It's on the level of feeling and vibration, our very being, and the standard in which you hold your being, which becomes our character. Everything stems from that place. Our thoughts, deeds, actions, choices, and life. The quality and caliber of our life. The amount of joy you feel bursting through your very being all the days of your life and more.

All from the things no one ever knows or sees. The level of your feelings and honoring your feelings. The feelings beyond the feelings into the depth of feeling itself. We are not talking about the frivolous feelings that come and go, nor the thoughts or actions, but the deeper intention of holding your inner space with the utmost regard and care, which means doing the inner work. Through this continual release and ease, everything naturally comes to be. Where love springs forth in greater full force, where peace and passion come to dance and play, and then the tremendous joy makes its way to say hey!

For what is the true measure of success?

Is it money, fame, or anything tangible and of this world? No. True success is true, unbridled joy. When we feel that, we've connected to the very essence of our being. For you are that. Yes, you are that which you have been seeking all along. It's already within. It's already there. It's already burning, pulsing, and growing. Our inner voice, our consciousness, our heart.

And with heart, regardless of our level of consciousness at the time, this is how we expand and awaken our awareness, and vice versa. Regardless of our level of awareness at the time, this is how we expand and awaken our consciousness. Our conscious awareness and our aware consciousness grow significantly, and we pop into our heart or higher consciousness and let innate wisdom flow. For love is just that. There is nothing greater than love. There is nothing greater than the truth of who you are, for you are this great love, too.

Yes.

You are this great love you have been seeking and searching for. It's you, not outside of you, but within you, as you, simply you.

Speaking of happiness and peace, everyone wants peace if they do because some don't. That's the truth of it. We're not ready until we're ready, and there is no judgment, shame, or blame in this for self or others. Reflecting on our lives, we find the compassion to begin understanding. Ahh, yes, I see now. Back then, I was not ready to hear the truth; I was not ready to begin. I was not ready for any of this. Or I could not see? That's okay, though.

Every period of our lives is needed, or else it simply would not be. There is no shame in this. It is grace and bliss as well. That is the journey. Of not just you but consciousness. How can it grow if we do not live?

And live we shall.

Suppose you've been at this for a while. In that case, you've already gone down the rabbit hole of personal development, psychology, philosophy, and even the spiritual side. I understand that. I did, too. I always believed in being open to listening to new ideas, thoughts, approaches, ways, people, modes, and modalities and making up our minds on what resonates with us in our lives and in our way of being, not just with this, but anything and everything.

So, on this journey, regardless of where we may find ourselves in our exploration, often the truth presented in whatever form is jam-packed. It's a lot to take in and process, depending on where we are within ourselves. This thought used to cross my mind. How was I going to learn it all? But you don't even have to worry if you're absorbing it all fully because we only pick up what we are vibrationally ready for, aka like attracts like. We pick up the golden nuggets best for us at that moment as the you that you are, simply perfect to and for your person, which propels you to your next level of being. In this way, everything is taken care of.

You do not need to worry if you're doing a good job, if you're not doing enough, if you're not getting it all, or just whatever the mind thinks of to try and pull you down into the energy of less than.

All is truly well.

So, you want to know how to attain your highest ideal?

You start with where you are.

Yes. That's it. It's that simple. Let alone it's the best any one of us can humanly do in life. Should we choose to honor the loving way and live by and through one's heart, miraculous doors open up, both within and without. The kind fairy tales are made of. This, I promise.

And in a nutshell, that is the journey.

I honor you on your journey.

The Story of All Humanity

This has been the journey of humanity since the dawn of time itself. It always has been. It is even now. It shall continue to be so till the very end of time itself and long after that, for love truly is eternal.

How each generation and group of souls brings forth their energy, the energy of their unique being. Then, together, as we share ourselves and our energy, our heart, and our love with the world, we shape and reshape this world, from the very micro events to world events, by our energy alone, for every action is the consequence of our internal state. In this way, every person contributes to the welfare of all mankind simply by the power of their love, the alignment and use of their energy, and their inner landscape. We don't think it plays a part or a role, and we don't think we play a part or a role, but fundamentally, it does, and you do. That's how powerful every person is.

World peace begins at home at the doorstep of our mind and being. As we calm our minds, release our hearts, and unleash our souls, we naturally raise our vibration and approach and face life differently, simply because we are whole new people. That's how profound vibrational shifts are. That's how profound the energy of love is. That's how profound the truth of who you are is.

Let's face it: whenever we finally release a limiting belief, no matter how big or small it may be, because it has been practiced for quite some time, it's always a big release within our being. It feels that way. It's a new breath of fresh air for you and everyone. As we step out into the world, we become the light for others, not because we want to or have to, but because we naturally are.

Often, or at times, we think life is unfair. We wonder why this happened to us, if things were different, if I wasn't born this way, if I was born into a different family, or whatever story we tell ourselves repeatedly. What it comes down to is choice. Even before that, to learn that we even have a choice. Choice in the matter to choose anew always in all things. A new path. A new thought. A new way. A new way of being. Simply a new you. Yes. When we claim our power and step into the truth of who we are and the more of who we are, the outcome is simply endless, boundless, and bountiful.

We always have a choice in everything. Yet sometimes, we forget because we are all only human. As we lean into our faith over fear, choices naturally emerge. The choice to choose a better way. The choice to choose kindness.

Kindness toward others but, most of all, self. The choice to choose love. The choice to choose joy. The choice to live, whatever that may mean for you. Not the living you have been doing, but the kind of living that excites your being, calls to you, and hence takes you higher. When you finally choose, things get clear, noticeably clear, if not crystal clear.

Our entire life is about choice. You are a creator, the creator of your reality. The magician, the alchemist, the miracle worker. For when we finally choose with heart, therein lies the miracle. The miraculous, if not deciding, choice and factor for each person on how they want to live, who they want to be, and how they want to show up within themselves and the world. It's always both. Our external reality is always a reflection of our internal reality.

So, with that said, as we work on ourselves, we create ripple effects just in our being alone. Then, the energy we align with creates more ripple effects. It's endless how one drop can affect the entire ocean, as the ocean affects the drop. We are tied and bonded, deeper than blood, but by spirit.

If one chose compassion, kindness, consideration, and care, if one chose love, what a difference it would be. A monumental difference in your life and the course of your life, and by extension, your world and the world at large. For we are all connected, and we are all one.

We strengthen each other, or we weaken each other.

We lift each other, or we break the bond that ties.

But what no one thinks about,

Is how that bond is inextricable.

For it simply is like all that is.

Simply and just as you are.

Some things can never be broken.

And that is one of them.

You and your spirit.

You and your light.

You and your love.

You and all humanity

You and all divinity.

These are the eternal truths.

We are all connected, and we are all one.

And it doesn't matter what your faith may be.

No one can deny the miracle of life.

The miracle, that is.

The miracle that you are.

The miracle that unites us all.

We have air in our lungs and a heartbeat in our chest.

What is that force that keeps us going?

Is that not a miracle in itself?

And as we raise our consciousness, we raise our collective consciousness. It's like a melting soup, a melting pot of energy. Each person's heart and soul play a part in the great soup of life, where the depth of love can be born and birthed from a higher vantage point, taking us all further, higher, and deeper than ever.

And as more people choose themselves, love, or peace. They choose it for all humanity by simply working on themselves. Having the courage to work on ourselves, we assist all mankind to do the same, simply in vibrational being alone. Anything else you choose to do is a gift to the world. For now, you are in vibrational sync and harmony with the truth of who you are, and you give it. Your deepest love. Your very love. Simply all your love. In whatever endeavor you choose, champion, or even enjoy.

For now, it is about the true enjoyment of what is. No more filters. No more distractions. No more contractions. Simple, pure, and true. It is all of you. In all of it. The work of your life. To be you. Do you. And give your love. Life is that simple. Nothing else matters.

Our collective energy adds to the whole through this service, the service of your own life and your joy. We raise the awareness and consciousness of all humanity. Yes, it is a service, but it is also an honor and a privilege to be here now in this time and place as you are. Remember that.

For in every way, this is the utmost truth, for your life is sacred, sacred space and sacred ground for the sacred to sing through and resound.

I lovingly hold this faith for you, for I know this to be true without any doubt; you are that, that which you are.

For one person meets another meets another. We all meet at different times and places, given who we are and where we are now. This has always been true, but now there will be more grace, peace, and presence. The true grace and beauty of this. There are no words for the divine beauty of all that is and all that you are—and then meeting together in this way. What a true honor to have an effect or be affected by those you meet and share a precious moment.

And so, with each generation, as more courageous people, people like you choose to love, choose themselves, peace, joy, faith, and kindness. Together, we affect this world for now; when we meet others, we will not pass down the unconscious behavior of our forefathers and generations past; the cycle of soul violence or unconscious doing stops with you. With you, you birth a new karmic seed and cycle within and to those you touch, and ever so sweetly, grace is birthed anew.

That is the profound effect and miracle called you, life, and all of the above. That is the healing power of love, and that is the healing power of who you are. Lastly – that is – who you are.

You are love.

Every person's path, be it what it may, is the same path. To claim our love. To be this love. To give and offer this love to ourselves and the world. That is the highest goal. The highest joy. The highest honor. The highest honor one can ever attain is to be and breathe. For the honoring of our love is its reward. The birthing of our beauty and contributing to our collective beauty at large and scale, starting with you, dearest. Yes. You.

Just to be ourselves true.

For it took you to begin the chain reaction.

Of healing, growth, self-discovery, and love.

God bless you for all that you do.

God bless you in your journey.

God bless you, my love.

There may be no one else who understands this passion.

But I do.

And I honor you.

You are not alone.

For we are all in this together.

You, me, and all humanity.

This above all. I know for sure, dearest.

This I know to be true.

We are kindred, you and I.

Keep faith.

And love shall have its day.

For it already has.

In our hearts.

It is simply a matter of time.

And because of you and our collective consciousness, we raise the vibration of humanity not just now but for all time to come. Just think about it. One more person who doesn't feel so bad about themselves. That's profound if not a darn miracle. That's the energy they give and offer the world because they choose to work on themselves.

When we work on our healing, we heal the world.

CHAPTER THREE

The Journey

"Love yourself first, and everything else falls into line. You really have to love yourself to get anything done in this world." — *Lucille Ball*

The Journey of Awakening in a Nutshell

This is the most natural journey and experience of our life. It's inevitable. All we have to do is live, and eventually, life will throw us curve balls that will inspire us to desire more, whether that be more clarity, peace, joy, well-being, centeredness, resolve, strength, understanding, or more love. Whatever it is, it simply is.

We may or may not act upon these newfound desires right away. Still, eventually, we all begin to look within because it dawns on us that the only way to find happiness is by working on ourselves, body, mind, heart, and soul. It's a lot. Yet who doesn't want more joy in their lives? And deeper than joy, underneath every desire is a deeper desire we have yet to name but always resides.

Do we want the new house, job, or promotion for what it is or will give us? And what does an abundance of any form and kind bring? More time, freedom, and opportunity to share and enjoy with loved ones. For what purpose does that pose? Simply for more love and joy! Love, self-love, and love all around.

We may not specifically call it the journey of awakening, but inadvertently, it is. Whenever we go within to find, create, and release a measure of peace, love, or any goodness we endeavor upon within or without, that is the journey. It is the release of who we are.

Any true heart endeavor brings about this, an awakening of a kind. As we continue to honor our hearts and align with the depth of who we are, our deeper wants, desires, dreams, and more naturally come about. We spend a lifetime seeking the kind of illumination we've yearned for simply by living, being, and being true to you.

This is the true beauty and the grace of humanity and what it simply is. By living, we are guided if we only listen to our heart. We're guided regardless, but it's all always there and only magnified. One can only smile in joy and glee if not sheer reverie, as we feel this sacred truth.

Every person you meet is on the journey of a lifetime, the journey of their heart and soul, the journey to come alive. How beautiful it is; as we allow what we allow and see what arises and comes forth from within and without, it's always the beauty of who we are that shines. On this path, life, and journey, we never do anything alone, nor do we ever walk this walk alone, no matter how alone we may be. Faith and trust are like beautiful angel dust. Our heart connects us to the Heavens and beyond, to the universe and beyond, to humanity and beyond, to eternity and beyond, and to all divinity and beyond. Our heart is the central gateway to everything. Everything possible, imaginable, unimaginable, and more beyond that. There is simply no end to the more of all that is, is already, and is right now. Then, yes, more, even beyond that.

So, to honor and appreciate everyone you meet. Wherever they are, they are. Just as you were where you were all those many years ago and are right now, we are where we are, or else it would not be, and that's okay. However, we may feel about it when we can release critical judgment of self, we can release it from others, and no longer do you hold yourself or others in conscious or unconscious bondage and behavior. Or when we can live in compassion for ourselves, we can show it to others. For we emanate who we are, and that is what we give. Let alone lightening up on yourself and giving others the freedom to be what a profound and priceless gift for that takes actual presence. Either way. All humanity, every person you ever meet, is on a sacred journey, the journey of their soul to the remembrance of the whole. The whole of all that they are and the whole of all that is.

And regarding change and bettering our lives, we all want change if and when we do, but sometimes we don't, and that's perfectly fine, too. If you're happy and things are going well, why on Earth would anyone want change? And rightfully so! That is the perfect place to be for that is pure alignment. As we live and grow, eventually, we all come across the desire to make peace, release our conditioning, and reach for the depth of being one way or another.

Then, of course, when we are sad, it becomes clear that something must change. I must change. I don't know what it is, but I'm willing to find out now; I'm willing to try now, you tell yourself, and you mean it with all your heart. We're only ready when we're ready. As we reflect upon our lives, we begin to see how true this was for you on your path.

And then, for some of us, regardless of the joy or the pain, or through a deeper desire or yearning, we may even want to awaken, achieve enlightenment, and know the highest version of ourselves where we are free. The kind of freedom that many have spoken to and spoken for and spoken about for centuries on end. If it was true back then, is it possible that it can be true now? Can it be true for me? Can it be my reality? You begin to wonder and dream.

Dream about joy, ecstasy, bliss, and pure fulfillment in this life and lifetime. The love that Rumi had, can it burn in my soul too? And deep down, that's all of us. Whether we consciously ask ourselves, that's what we all want. Who doesn't have the innate desire to better themselves and their lives and finally know what it means to live and come alive? To a love beyond love beyond love itself.

Not the living you see on TV or social media where everything is portrayed and displayed as if it were a parade, but the living where you feel it in your soul, pulsing with joyous play. Deeper than your heart, or rather together with your heart, your heart is so open; you feel it burning in your soul, dancing free, dancing in wild ecstasy. To feel the complete sheer and total gratitude of the joy of being and living is simply the joy of it all. Now, words like love, gratitude, and joy are more than words but carry weight and take on a life of their own, for they are synonymous with your name, no matter what happens.

Yes. Come what may.

That's saying a lot because that means you will honor your heart, whatever that may mean, and be for you. You will honor the love you know to be true even if you may or may not know what that is quite fully. So, you will honor how you feel the best you know how. That means honoring self, aka self-love. So be it so you say.

You have grown enough now to see it through, regardless of cost, for there is no more significant cost than your joy and the great fire of love that burns in your soul. This fire fuels both your peace and your passion and keeps you warm all the days of your life. This is the great fire that lit the night sky since the dawn of time itself, the eternal fire that warms even the coldest of all nights, which puts the sparkle and shine in someone's eyes that glistens as bright as the sun. That is something money can't buy. That's what all entertainment and media try to copy, convey, and capitalize on. To emulate, but that's all it is.

You know, when it's an act, or someone has found that special something, that intangible something, that special quality, that magic spark, that X factor, if you will, that sets them apart from all the rest. Are they any better or worse than you or anyone else? No. They just stopped pretending and started owning their truth, beauty, love, whatever that may mean. Genuine authenticity, beyond the word's meaning, is an energy everyone feels when it goes deeper into being. It touches them. After all, it releases them because, deep down, it is also who they are and a call to who they are. The rising of the phoenix within, the great love that drips with the purest love and sings like a dove. The rising tide that lifts and raises all mankind.

That is the power of pure, raw, unconditional presence. Presence of soul. Presence of heart. Presence of love. Yes.

But alas, we're only ready when we're ready to begin the inward journey. Yet, at the same time, our lives are in complete divine order, and all is as it should be. Is this not the journey, too? Then perhaps you are, we are, on that inward journey. Simply by living, all shall come to pass. Everything is genuinely inevitable for so many reasons. It becomes especially inevitable when we live by and from the heart. Then, it is done long before it has even begun. Everything was and is a vibrational reality before it manifests into this time and space reality.

But back to awakening.

This ideal has taken on many names, shapes, and forms throughout time, space, and culture. Simply, the honoring of life: our life and the honoring of all life, simply the honoring of love itself. Yes, it is a true honor to honor our love and give our love and joy. We all know people want this, but deeper than wanting it, it is an actual honor and a privilege.

Every faith, culture, and tradition express this beauty in its way. We may be called to a particular representation of this grace on display that calls out to us and more, the more profound longing in our soul that desires to be. If we boil it down, it is all the same. Living by and from the heart. Thereby releasing and being divinely wholly purely you. Yes, radically you. Whatever that may mean.

And is it so radical, or is it the most natural?

The whole point to finding peace in this life and doing our inner work, aside from the benefits it already brings, is this. As we release all old behaviors and pockets of insecurity that arise within, it clears and creates the space for more to show up; the more to arise within, the more to finally begin.

That more is you, buried deep within. Like the phoenix rising from the ashes of all that is old to claim the whole of all that is. All that is good, all that is true, and all that is you. There's simply a lot to who you are and the depth of who you are.

So then. What is that perennial question?

Who am I?

That is the question of a lifetime that one can ponder eternities. In truth, all you have to do, is just be you. Lovingly, look in the mirror and appreciate yourself. That energy creates and calls a profound beginning of true alignment and connection to self and soul. Once we have a clearer connection, once you've cleared the things that no longer serve to any margin or degree, or instead, as we continue to do our inner work, for that is truly a lifelong journey for anyone, nothing is blocking you from you anymore. The depth of you. Your deepest wishes, desires, and dreams.

Simply you.

And the very heart of you.

To find the wellspring of love that is always flowing and flowing, constantly bubbling, and singing, and overflowing to all the parts and places of your being, both within and without, and into your time and space reality. That is a clear representation of reality. When you see with the eyes of absolute love, love unconditionally. Love all around. Love that reverberates and resounds.

Love is the highest vibration there is, let alone the only thing that is. As we cultivate this space within us, release, realize, and recognize this space within us, this love connects us to the great beyond. Whatever our faith, our love connects us to the depths of all eternity, humanity, and divinity. Simply everything.

For there is nothing that love does not touch.

And yes, you are a part of this great love.

You are this great love.

It burns within you.

Waiting to come through.

And in truth, it already does.

And as we do our inner work and heal all the broken, scary places, this eventuality is even more so.

The birthing of love itself.

As you.

Frequently, though, especially in the spiritual community, all you see are people meditating or doing yoga or talking about meditating and doing yoga. Where is love and the many discussions of how it burns in your soul like nothing has ever been done before, the fire that returns you to the fullness and wholeness of all that is? Aka, the opening of one's heart.

When people think spiritual, that's all they think of and nothing more. They think it's about learning to silence your mind versus the actual deep, vibrant coming alive. They think it's something outside of themselves or something airy-fairy and not for them. They think it's about people just sitting around singing kumbaya and not doing anything with their lives. They think about it as an idea versus the tried-and-true visceral reality that takes your breath away.

And for some, it's only about taking pictures of yourself meditating or doing yoga versus doing meaningful, soul-enriching work. There is nothing wrong with this, for we are where we are, and we resonate with what we resonate, for it's all a choice on how we choose to live our life.

Meditating is essential, and there is a whole yogic philosophy behind this. This is true. This is true. This is why. Yet, there are many paths to the same place and more ways to grace than one can ever name. Being spiritual is not a label or an idea, phrase or phase, philosophy, ideology, or any of that; it is deeper than all. It is who you are. It's your nature. It's how we live and breathe. It's how we function. It's an innate function of being, just like breathing. If we only listened to our hearts, it is so. Spirituality is not something you do; it's something you are.

The whole point of finding peace, the spiritual path, and the inward journey is that you contact the passions of your soul: or simply the joy, the aliveness, the fire, the vibrancy, simply the light. From the peace or the stillness you allowed and created through your inner work comes the passion, either a true passion or simply the passion for life and living that burns. The kind of fire that lights you afire. The conviction or curiosity that propels you to take inspired action as you choose what good to bring into your life.

Nothing is in your way anymore. All the noise is gone. All the lower blocks, lesser patterns, and less than emotions are gone. You are in the ground of your being, and what a wondrous place that is. Now, your true nature, essence, and heart call out to you and speak to you so you can hear, feel, taste, touch, smell, and know to be true. The divine in you that's been given a chance to sing to you and sing it does.

What do they say?

They can say any number of things.

Let's create some awesome code, do some gardening and knitting, write that book, create a play or a movie, take stand-up comedy, start singing, pick up guitar lessons, and get that engineering degree I always wanted.

Whatever it is, it is. We all have different passions, joys, loves, interests, curiosities, and callings that speak to us. We all enjoy different things, and that is wonderful because that is what we each have to bring, share, and give to ourselves and the world. Our pure joy as we discover and experience it for ourselves.

More than the idea and the image, if not a caricature of meditating all day, spiritual means doing you, going after you, being you, giving you, and loving yourself enough to be yourself true. This is the true definition of self-love.

Sure, meditation comes into play, if not highly essential, as it allows you to hear the deeper callings of your being. Still, spirituality is about living and experiencing your life in every way, shape, and form, especially all your dreams and desires, simply your every joy. Pure desire is how the energy of the world pours through. Just look at yourself. You know this to be true. Just look at how far you've come. It wasn't just wishing it all into existence per se; you acted.

The only difference is it was inspired action. You moved with the energy of your soul versus the energy of brute force alone. Before that action could begin, you allowed the wishing of your desires and dreams to move your being, which then took you to new emotional heights within. The exploration of what could be and could be for you. This is what you would call the allowing.

Whereas most people would talk themselves out of it or say it is impossible or simply silly. They cut themselves off before they have even begun. Have you noticed how often we do that until we catch ourselves and become clear on various limiting beliefs hiding in the unconscious nooks and crannies of our being and then lovingly say goodbye? There was a time when that served, but no longer. Then, with that addressed, you allow it to continue to grow like a snowball, all your hopes, cultivating it lovingly tenderly and warmly within the bosom of your being. Now, with the vibrant states of possibility, openness, and inspiration come forth all the ideas and clues, new realities waiting to be born, and a new you waiting to embrace it all and see it through.

It's not about playing a role or a part of whatever we're supposed to be, look like, or be categorized as. Even for one labeled and deemed as spiritual, which takes on so many connotations in this day and age, or even any label at all for that matter. No. It's about breaking all the conceived and preconceived ideas and creating anew from your new stance within yourself, as yourself, and your true self. Was this self different from the old self? No. Not at all. The only difference was heart. More heart. The release of heart. The opening of one's heart. Which then empowers all you do.

Your heart was always there. It's what's guided you all along, dearest. Now, there is a measure of a kind, a caliber of a sort, of strength, fire, courage, grit, faith, compassion, and pure joy—any person who taps into these qualities, is their true self. As our heart expands, so do all these qualities along with the natural gifts and talents born to us. We're meant to share these gifts with the world because we could share them with ourselves first; this is the gift you get to live into.

So yes, some think the idea of being spiritual is to meditate. Granted, that has a significant place and part to play. True spirituality is the coming alive of one's spirit and soul and to release the whole. The whole of you and the whole of all that is. The fire of our love in whatever fashion and form. That is bliss and ecstasy. When we are ourselves unleashed.

So, how do we begin the journey of awakening? Many overcomplicate this, intellectualize this, and overdo it. However, it's simple. You need only three things to begin the greatest journey there ever was, is, and shall be. Not just now but for all time to come.

To Begin the Awakening

To Begin

Everyone says they want to change, but change is impossible if these three energies aren't present within. In truth, this applies to all kinds of beginnings. Any venture one desires: business, school, or simply awakening to the truth of who you are.

You need three energies within you. Desire. Openness. Willingness.

Defined as:

DESIRE – TO WISH OR LONG FOR, CRAVE, WANT.

OPENNESS – THE QUALITY OF BEING RECEPTIVE TO NEW IDEAS. OPEN-MINDEDNESS.

WILLINGNESS – CONSENT OR READINESS TO DO SOMETHING.

What is so important about these three energies?

I know the distinction might be minute to some and ever so subtle, but it is monumental and plays a role.

Let's dive in.

Desire

The entire world is born of desire. Anything you see was once but a wonderful dream in someone's daydream, vivid imagination, or at the heart of their being. Their desires manifest. The energy of desire is like fuel, the energy required to push things through from thought form to a tangible reality.

The energy of desire energizes and catalyzes the rest of our being to align and realign itself to meet this desire and its goal. That's how strong it is, and that's how powerful it is. This is how the universe works. People always talk about the law of attraction. Still, if we break it down, this is it: pure desire and alignment to one's desires, aka oneself.

And the purer the desire, the truer the desire, the more potent the fire, if it's a heart and soul desire, well then, you have mighty energies working for you and with you in the endeavor of your choosing and the endeavor of your life.

Just think, once a desire is born, whatever it may be, it's like a little Napoleon Bonaparte being born within. A little Napoleon Bonaparte bunny with all the resources needed to command to your attention what is needed and call it forth and draw it forth from yourself and the world. For like attracts like. Of course, your little Napoleon is not a dictator wanting to take over the world but more so a dynamic, playful energy coming in response to the whole, the energizer bunny that keeps going and going and going.

The whole of you asked, and the whole of you is answering.

With the inner resources abundant and resplendent.

Yours for taking and picking, plucking, munching.

Revitalizing. Rejuvenating. Renewing.

Simple you and simply yours.

It's as simple as that.

Your little Napoleon is in service to the whole.

And is in service to you.

For it is the energy of the soul.

And this energy is connected to the whole of life itself.

It is a dynamic energy fueled with desire; your Napoleon can command legions, all the legions within and without, to do what must be done, the fulfillment of the calling of your heart and soul, the fulfillment of your higher whole, the fulfillment that has arisen within your being.

When Admiral Yamamoto spoke those famous lines during Pearl Harbor, "I fear we have awakened the sleeping giant" concerning America? Even Napoleon himself said something similar about China over two hundred years ago. A great power lies within, dormant yet ever ready, when called upon and when needed. That power lies within us all.

When we wake up in a sense and mobilize and catalyze all that we are in service for the greater good, need, calling, desire, and the greater fire within us, that desire must be met. You will put your life into it. Not because you have to but simply because this is what you must do.

It is a must-do because your soul moves and desires you to do so. So the energy is not a forceful bully, dictator, or a forceful push; it's not coming from a place of lack, less than, or hustle culture, but more so, it's almost an effortless gentle push and lifting, lifting of one's soul and being to do what must be done and to live to the calling of your soul that has arisen and awakened!

It takes and is a great honor to listen to the calling of one's being, the calling of one's life. It is a true privilege to be here now, in this plane and reality, in this time and space, as you are on Earth today. You are the gift you have been waiting for. You are the gift the world has been waiting for. You are the gift all Heaven has been waiting for. It has always been you and not anyone or anything outside of you. It's always been within.

And by honoring this call, our joy, our love, in whatever fashion and form, you truly serve yourself and all mankind. You get rewarded as such by immeasurable means. The joy and the overwhelming love that now beats loud and free in your chest is undeniable; no one can ever take away your connection to yourself and your soul. No one can break asunder your connection to Him alone: to the Divine in all of us, to the Divine in all that is, to the Divine that is.

Now, with desire, desire can be tricky.

Outwardly, two people may be doing the same thing born from desire, some outward push, momentum, or action. Still, one has the power of their soul, and all that is working with them as they move with effortless ease, grace, and flow.

And the other? Well. We are all familiar with what that one's like. When you push and pull, you relentlessly hustle to try and force things through, like trying to put a square peg in a round hole. It's not as dynamic, strong, and aligned as possible. While both actions may get the work done. One was at ease, and one was pulling teeth. One invigorates and energizes, while the other saps and seeps at your energy much more rapidly, leaving you drained. One is grace and flow, and one is hustle and strain. Oh, let us not live in vain!

But it's all right, for all life is but practice. Practice and awareness. Are we aligned? Are we true? If these are yes, then awareness grows regardless. If the desire is pure, if a pure desire has genuinely been born within, naturally, we align ourselves with our wanting as we open our hearts and allow ourselves to feel these new feelings, taking us further than we've ever been. The act of feeling our desire is an actual act of courage as well.

You must open your heart, despite your fear, and feel into this new reality. To dream a dream only you can dream. Thus allowing the opening for the bud to take root and blossom within good and divine time into the ethers of all space and time.

Often, we do not see it that way or can't see much of it at all. Still, when the energy clears, you begin to see what is there—the purity of your desire that reignites your fire, which opens your heart and makes you start.

Which begins a new journey as well.

Desire is fuel and fire.

Openness

As coaches say, you must remain coachable. As monks say, you must have open hands, not closed and clenched hands. An open hand is synonymous with an open mind and heart, simply an open cup. How can your cup take on more if it is full of water? If it's empty, then you can receive more. It's similar to how we approach anything, let alone ourselves and our lives. Only from there are we willing to see, feel, be, and try. Not merely an endeavor but the sheer experience of our life!

It's about being open and receptive to new ideas versus being closed off with either a know-it-all attitude or any less-than attitude, being open-minded, as they say. Which also means not just being open to new ideas but also to old ones too. Finally, being able to confront them, be mindful of them, and be present with them. Your deeds, thoughts, emotions, feelings, micro feelings, and the space in between the feelings. Simply, yourself in full.

Yes. Simply being a watcher of our internal world and dialogue and getting curious versus critical. The world of emotion is a separate entity and, left unwatched, can pillage and ravage from us our resources, our lives, and the quality and caliber of our lives. It can take from you the things you need to build a successful life, a life you love, a life you dream.

And yet, what is success but a heart's content? A heart that has realized itself. A heart that has found its home or is simply on the way there, on the opening journey. There is no greater joy than one's heart and soul journey. There is no greater joy than being who you indeed are. There is no greater joy than to be. When you know you are in it, you become fully alive, engaged, and excited to embrace the day.

Because every new experience, every new moment, every new breath, is the moment that can turn it all around, that very aha you've been looking for or a moment of genuine appreciation that opens your being ever so subtly, the answer that will take you to the next level, the next level of your heart and soul and person with new integration and a piece of distinction and learning. It's like the flower of your soul growing, breathing, and learning to open and root, stand, come alive, and learn to be.

But first, we must be open. I know the idea of facing ourselves is not ideal sometimes. Let alone, what on Earth does that even mean, some might ask. Most simply, it means being open enough to look at things differently, from a different perspective, in a new light—both the good and bad things, all things.

Ok, I get what you're saying, but what if I still can't? Some of my friends have been seeing a therapist, and it never gets better; some are seeing a therapist, and they do. Yes, that's a journey with many factors, for each person and therapist has their own way of life and being.

Or a dream is so big, it feels so impossible, so ridiculous, so insane, I feel so small and inadequate. Yes, who hasn't felt that way before, and isn't that how it's supposed to be, a dream that completely excites you and pushes you toward your greatest reality, the person you are meant to be? Every dream is born for a reason. Allow the experience of such a dream to marinate, simmer, and stew in your being.

But in general, yes. Sometimes, when we can't release it or are stuck, we feel less than ourselves. It's best to shake that energy off and do anything that changes the tone, like talking to a good friend you trust, taking a long walk or jogging in the park, listening to soothing music, or even writing out your thoughts.

The point is, now we are simply willing enough to be open enough, not just to our likes and particulars, but our dislikes as well, simply everything. We are open enough to what is, whatever that may mean, and that is a powerful jumping-off point. That is true receptivity. Open to within, open to without.

We often look at our peers or those in our lives, and they say they hate this and that. Look at what the energy of hate and all those thoughts is costing and bringing them, regardless of whatever "right" reason. Sometimes, the energy of obstinance and obstacles grows and hardens itself like an invisible wall and magnifies through our intense focus, which then inflates the reality and situation that closes our eyes to be able to see, except that which we want to see, which then continues to justify our reality and perception of reality and our identity within that reality.

Then, without meaning to, all the things we hate or dislike become our guiding light and focus because that's where we pour our energy and attention. That becomes our energetic, emotional base and what we attract into our lives. It's all subconsciously done. It's so slight because these are feelings and emotions, down to the subtle layer below that of instinct, gut, and practiced energetic patterns.

And well, thoughts are thoughts; yes, it's true. Each thought has a certain quality of energy associated with and tied to it. If you will, a pull of gravity attracts power, which then begins to root, seed, and grow. Deepening itself into your ecosystem, the ecosystem of your heart, soul, and mind. Hence, your life.

Simply being open to looking at things another way. Or being open to looking and being observant in general to the conditioning of our mind and the way it responds or the way it's triggered and the way it likes and dislikes, abhors, and enjoys. Lastly, simply being open to genuine desires and whatever arises—all of it.

If we are open to all of it, open to all that is, if our heart is finally open, how can it not come?

Openness is receptivity and possibility.

Willingness

What good is it to want something and be open to it but unwilling to try?

Everyone wants to go on that diet to lose 20-30 lbs. It's so financially lucrative, and we see commercials everywhere because it's a common theme and problem many of us want to address. Or how everyone wants to quit drinking or smoking, or whatever it is we want to address. Sure, we mentally want to do this because we intellectually know it's good for us and would help us out overall. We don't act toward this until we are finally ready, get honest with ourselves, and become genuinely ready and willing. The desire might be genuine, and you might be open to the idea versus dismissing it, but without being ready and willing, desire and openness get you nowhere.

The analogy of the coach and monk applies here, too. If your cup is full, how can you receive more? But once we are open to the ideas of all ideas. The ones that call out to you toward your higher growth. You must be willing to dip your toes in the water regardless of whether you have swum before. You must be willing to ride that bicycle to get into the cycle of things. You must be willing to ride the roller coaster if you want the ride of your life. We must consent to the new idea presented before us.

New fads, trends, or gimmicks always occur within every industry. Think about all the fitness fads, healthy diets, and the latest workout equipment promised to deliver results and change your life. They are all a dime a dozen. In reality, are we ready? Are we willing to plunge in and commit? Are we willing to stick it through? Are we willing to try it out? You were open to the idea, who isn't, but were you truly willing?

How it might be what we want, but are we willing to do it? We've all been there. I'll do it, work on it, and start it tomorrow. The mind says yes, but not 100%. If the mind says yes, but the rest of you don't, then no. We're not fully committed. We're not fully in it. We're not fully invested. There is no willingness.

Whatever your answer may be, it's okay. Much like anything else, it's where we are at the moment, which can change in the next moment. For one, true constant is change. Naturally so because we, too, are simply that vast and that dynamic. Forever, we are growing and evolving in every way possible, mentally, emotionally, physically, and spiritually. Simply in every way, it is the nature of the heart and soul to do so, to simply be.

When it's time, when it clicks, we get that internal gut pull that says, yes, I must try this now. No one can pinpoint or say when that moment is. It's different for everyone. All these motivational speakers and leaders may pump you up and down for one purpose. Still, if we're not ready, if we're not there, or if we are unwilling, no amount of hype, smooth-talking, or even helpful, factual advice will help. It is not the time through no fault of anyone. It's just not time.

When it clicks, it clicks, and when it hits, it hits. Then, you know. It's time. Things are going out of control, and you realize you have to snap out of it. Or you've fulfilled many things, but something is still missing. Or you are sensitive to emotions, and it's gut-knowing. Either way. When it's time, it's time, and then you know. It is time.

We all get that feeling from time to time for any number of things, from the big to the small. It's about being receptive to it and acting. Sometimes, it takes being unhappy or stuck in a certain way within ourselves for the dissatisfaction or the pain to reach a threshold or some event that tells us it's time. Only to realize without our past way of being, we never could have reached this new level of insight that takes us to the next. Where we are ready to sit with ourselves, be honest with ourselves, and make changes.

Let us not judge ourselves for not being here or there or wherever our mind thinks we should be. This is a journey.

Let us give ourselves the gift of the freedom to be where we are, just as we are. This is called grace. Yes. Grace can be profound, and grace can be profoundly simple, too. Something so simple no one thinks of it. Because everyone always imagines it to be so huge and so big and so mind-blowing. Also, everyone wants to be there now, rather than simply being here now. Everyone needs to be seen as the expert, the hero, or the person who delivers results.

We are going to do something simple. We are going to allow grace into ourselves and our lives. By allowing ourselves to be as we are right now, in the here and now, at this moment in time, and it's okay. You are okay. We are okay. This is enough. You are enough. We are enough, and it's more than enough. It's always enough; we have everything we need right now.

I remember hearing this many moons ago, and not that I didn't believe this, but it was pretty unbelievable. It was a hard pill to swallow. How can little ole me be enough? How is being here now okay? How do I have everything I need right now? But because I was willing, open, and desired, I was willing to listen and play with those ideas and, more importantly, allow my feelings to gestate rather than shooing them away, seeing how they feel and resonate. Simply seeing what it's like for me inside. Because the person speaking this to me had accomplished and done so much, and more than their accomplishments, had achieved a way of being, a peace and a purity I deeply respected and admired, I was open to listening instead of shrugging it off, no matter how crazy it sounded.

That I – am enough.

That I – actually have all that I need within me.

That I – am in the right place and at the right time.

Any logical person would be like, yeah, right.

I was open and willing versus cynical.

The facts speak for themselves. Have you heard someone say that before? Facts are facts. Reality is reality. That is true. With what lens and perception of reality are you looking with and from? Are you looking from the lens of everything is hard and impossible, or are you looking from the lens of everything is a miracle, and so, are you? Whichever reality you choose radically defines not how you show up, not your reality, but your life down to how you live, show up, and approach your life. The caliber and the quality and the sheer joy of your life. Everything is affected.

So, facts may speak for themselves. Grace speaks for themselves, too. Grace is grace. Love is love. That is the truest reality there is. If not, the only reality there is. Then, with that acknowledgment, there may be facts, this is true, but then, there is divine grace spread through it all, that eventually it simply becomes higher information to lead you to greater understanding both within and without. This is how everything genuinely serves a purpose if we only let it.

You are not defined by these facts or by any certain perceived reality. All life is and does; it elevates and releases you into you, the more of you. That, by definition, is what a miracle is. When we align ourselves back to who we truly are, to choose love, to choose peace, to choose you. That is when a new path opens up as you step through with all the heart you have. From this choice comes profound effects that will forever last. It was a simple choice that took grace, faith, and much love.

Let alone, in life, have you just noticed? Many people accomplish and do so much, but some do. Do, do, do. There is no heart, ground, or meaning. Or there is too much force, like dumping a pool of water or throwing a vase to catch that tiny pesky mosquito buzzing at you all day. That tremendous force is utilized not poorly but not to its full potential.

There's nothing wrong with that too. That is the journey! Learning to manage, utilize, and become aware of our energy. Our life is the canvas of our sacred journey. Our emotional world becomes a canvas to paint from and birth the seeds of our reality. Who we are and who we become is the canvas of our ever-blooming love. We start from where we are, like any hero does, like any sage does, as any master does. You start with where you are and what you have. No matter what that is and what it looks like for you, it's always the right place for us all.

The right place for the more to enter into our lives and hearts, the knowingness of who we truly are, that we are profound, powerful, creative beacons of light meant to shine like never before. Then, no! Wait, you say! You're the creative one, not me. Then I say, when you have the power of your soul behind you, when you are open to your heart, when you are aligned to your core, all the resources you need and more show up. Inner resources and outer, for it simply all is.

And you might surprise yourself. The energy of our being is always dynamic, powerful, unique, compassionate, and creative. When you are energized for your purpose, passion, or true desire, your little Napoleon is on the job, the divine who hears the call, and your heart opens the doors to it all. Only to realize your little Napoleon is not so little.

But anyway, this was just a long way of saying it. Just have faith.

And the willingness of spirit plays a part in opening the way.

If we are not willing, how can anything come through?

Willingness is consent.

And on another level, willingness also holds the energy of thy will be done, amen. For it is both consent, release, and surrender all in one.

And so, we say.

Thy will be done.

Amen.

Closing

Those are the only three things you need for anything, but especially something such as awakening to one's higher potential, awakening to who you truly are, and awakening to the love that lasts.

Or simply getting out of pain, getting into joy, or whatever it is we are after, which all leads to the same place. The love after that. In the hereafter. In the here and now. Yes.

So. If you're ever stuck.

Just sit with yourself and take time to reflect.

Do I have this desire?

Am I truly willing?

Am I open?

The Universe's greatest secrets are, in fact, not so secret and are there for all. Right in front of our very eyes, right in front of our very nose, right in front of our very heart. It's amusing how it's always this way.

There is a flow—a flow to all things and a great flow that connects it all. The great flow of this world and how we all connect are intricately woven into everything.

And if these three energies live in you.

That, yes, you do desire the opening of love's grace.

That yes, you are willing to see it through.

Yes, you are open to doing what must be done.

Or simply even open to what is.

No matter what it may be.

Then. Have faith.
And trust.

If you've wondered how anyone's ever done it.

How all these brilliant people have done it.

How all these saints and sages of all time have done it.

It was three qualities, these three traits, these three energies.

That is how – they all began.

That is how we all begin.

For anyone – on the journey.

Let alone, just living will do it.

And also.

Water must always rise to its level.

That is law.

It's basic science, common language, common sense, basic basic.

It's so basic. I'm not even sure there's a word for basic basic.

But so, too, the same goes with the heart and soul.

If the requirements are met, so too, we cannot help but be swept.

Swept into the great current and undercurrent and over currents, too.

And come to find a place so miraculous, wondrous, and marvelous it is true.

For the first time in your entire life,

You will not have words.

And you will know the true meaning.

Of speechlessness.

A mind that is struck.

A heart that is struck.

A soul that is so struck.

You stopped.

To bear witness.

And bear care.

To the love

That is staring right back at you.

From you, for you, outside of you.

All around you.

Within you.

To the very point.

There is no more you.

And there is only.

All eternity.

This.

Is my one hope, dream, and wish for you.

Take heart.

Keep faith.

And know you are on the right track.

In the journey of your life.

If I had heard this back then, I may or may not have changed much, but at the same time, it would have come into my soul, and it would have given me more peace, more care and comfort, more heart, and hence, more faith and more strength. A renewed irresolute resolve to continue in the journey called my life.

And that is my hope for you.

If you too desire, desire what no one else desires, desire to awaken to the greatest secret of the land, pure and true, then:

You are well on your way.

Final Note

The level of consciousness of those reading this is of a vast range. Yet, regardless of our stage, it is still the same. That is how the master is forever the student, and the student is already the master, for it's all a matter of time. If time is irrelevant, if there is no such thing as time, for time is a man-made construct, then you begin to see how it's truly the soul who is living, breathing, and beating true, beating as you.

Like a flower going through its stages and cycles of growth, seeding, sprouting, rooting, sprouting more, budding, blossoming, reaching toward the direction of the sun, and then full bloom, and at the height of this bloom, to touch the essence of the nectar, ambrosia, you too can blossom.

Some say it's an aphrodisiac, and understandably so. The energy of the truth of who you are, love itself pouring through you, is always that profound. When love truly washes over you this way, one can never be the same. It radically changes your life and the perspective of your life, if not all reality itself. Yes, the very reality of your life. Love has finally been cultivated, born, and reborn within your heart. To know and touch the stillness. To know the evergreen of everbloom. The bloom with no end. The eternal sunrise with no end. The soul with no end, but at home with all eternity's end.

Body, mind, heart, and soul are aligned.

And we are home, we are here, we are present.

That place is real, and that place exists.

And that place is as commonplace as the sun in the day.

That is the journey.

That is forever the journey.

That is the eternal journey.

The journey of awakening.

The journey of consciousness.

The journey of love.

This is the greatest journey of all humanity.

That none can part.

And none can be a part.

And when we face it true.

Miracles abound for you.

Through and through.

To the point and the fact,

That no one may believe you.

Except for those that do.

Except those who've lived it, too.

Except those on the journey of their lives, too.

The beauty of love that shines.

And shines through every person, place, or thing alive. It's true.

The beauty is astounding and resounding.

I would say out of anything, a person can choose in life.

This, by far, is the greatest journey to make.

It is the only journey to make.

And it is the only thing we are doing beyond what we do.

It's for this and this alone.

The realization of love.

Loves grace as and in you.

Loves grace in all its hues.

Loves grace, forever in bloom.

Hm.

So.

Do you want to go on a journey with me?

To find and touch all eternity.

I promise.

It's going to be super fun.

And lastly, as poetic as all this may sound.

I will say we are more than polite people of poetry.

We are flesh and blood, entire body and fully embodied, emotions, heart, soul, and all.

To live this life completely and truthfully and give all that we have.

To devote our life to a just cause, a fulfilling cause, the cause of our calling.

Or even simpler put, to follow the joy of our soul.

It is this what it means to honor our life.

And to live a good life.

To honor our love.

To Continue the Awakening

To Continue the Unfolding

So, you've started your journey and are in it now. You've tasted the sunshine and miracles divine, simply the sublime that shines in you, the sublime that shines through all things. Yes, once you've tasted that, no one can ever return. It's like Pringles; once you pop, you can't stop.

First, I can't stress enough the monumental undertaking you make.

A decision like this carries repercussions that ripple throughout one's whole heart and soul and throughout all time and space, and our shared spatial reality of this world and the next, not only now but for all time to come. So, for this, I want to say.

Thank you, and God bless you.

For there is none like you. This, I can say and know to be true. For who will go against their nature to find their truest nature? To find peace and love everlast. Who will devote themselves in true devotion to the undertaking of love at last? All life is with you with everlasting grace and faith throughout all time and space. As is all heaven itself, all humanity walks with you also. My heart is with you, too.

Things change once we say yes. That firm yes in our heart and soul calling. We all know the difference when we say yes.

It's a vastly different feeling and nuance. When we finally say yes, the world may not have changed; outwardly, nothing may have changed. It's true, but you have. There is a fire in your eyes, a fire in your spirit, and a fire in your belly. A fire in your heart and soul that you released into your being as you allowed your heart to feel this and allow it through and accept it as true.

That is what it takes to claim anything. We must feel, own, and then allow it through. With something like this, it's a profound energy shift.

You begin to operate from a deeper level of awareness and consciousness because your sincere intention creates the way. Naturally, things will arise as they always do. We are beginning the journey of a lifetime, and saying yes is the first step when our heart says yes to ourselves. Our joy. Our journey. Our love. Regardless of whatever name, label, or lens you put on it. That is the journey of awakening. For love is simply coming back home.

No matter what sector in life we are placed in or our temperament, we may face inwardly. Regardless of what arises in our journey, whatever hiccup or challenge it may be, if we continue to open our hearts and ask the divine for assistance and hold the faith, higher information will be shown on the matter, which will dissolve the matter to even greater healing allowing you to rise above and rise higher into and with yourself.

And if one does not believe in the divine, a true heart calls. Those can never be denied, either. It means energetically you have opened your heart, which always has profound effects. In one sense, it's about alignment with what is, and from there, more doors open, which begins another sacred journey. So, whatever our faith may or may not be, it is all meant to be for all humanity. This is also the grace of what is. For we all find a way and the way meant for us specifically.

We must continually do only three things for the opening and ever-blossoming to continue, aside from living and breathing from and in the heart. Things will always arise both within and without. It's the nature of being human and the nature of being alive. Yet, how everything always takes us back to now, and how everything always takes us back to our heart.

Our inner work involves accepting ourselves and what is, making and creating peace with self and what is, and the unconditional love of self and what is, to the best of one's ability. That is it. This will continue the flow that will open the heart and soul to greater expansion and more.

There is genuinely divine grace to and of all things in life. If we look for it, it has the potential to cataclysmically, radically, and profoundly, if not fundamentally, open our hearts to the point one can never be the same again, and compassion becomes your one true name. That is the journey of love. In whatever form and face. That is the journey of love. Love gives. It is what love does. We must honor this voice and this calling if we innately, wholly truly feel this, for there is no greater honor than to give one's love. To give one's joy. To give at all. It is the greatest honor of a lifetime.

Acceptance of Self and What is

One of the most challenging things is to accept ourselves and what is.

Challenges always have a way to poke and prod all the little pockets of insecurity. Yet that's what they are, merely pockets of insecurity that bubble up to the surface of our being. That is all. We all have areas of growth and unconsciousness, and life reveals it to us through the events in our lives. However, if we're willing to breathe through it and feel and face it the best we can, there is a release of a kind.

When we accept something, we may or may not like it. Still, we can better tolerate it within our emotional being to begin to move forward. It releases us from paralysis and helplessness and gives us the freedom of choice and mobility to act and choose for ourselves. When we accept things, there is no longer an energetic hold per se or, at the very least, a decreased hold.

It might sting occasionally, but we can better breathe through it and not let it energetically pull us down as it once had into unconscious behavior and patterns. We're not as immediately triggered as we once were. When we can accept things, it creates space for more. More of you to show up and more of all that is to come through. Simply more.

Acceptance of self and what is, or at the very least the intention to do so, almost eases the edges of one's emotional jagged pain that often feels like spiked balls ready to prick you on the slightest movement. Accepting and breathing through dulls the edges enough that despite whatever it may be, we can better handle and tolerate what is. This gives you a greater strength, ability, and resolve to manage what may come. It gives you a base, ground, and level within to stand on, work upon, and work fully through.

The moments when you want to crumble inside. After you've given in to the emotions, let out a few tears if you have to. We're all humans. Who hasn't faced those emotions and been there before? We all have. Anyone who tells you they haven't, it's just not true, or they have emotionally avoided going there and numbed themselves to themselves. Humans are human, and emotions are something no one can escape.

Let alone; it's through walking through the fires of those emotions, the fires of our inner demons, and the fires of all and every kind, if we are simply brave enough to face what is both within and without, a tremendous force is released. Our fears and trapped emotions are like trapped energy. We all have great stores of energy and even greater, richer, deeper stores within as we align with the truth of who we are. That is what we call soul force. As we work through our emotions and face and accept them, it releases the trapped energy and lets it return to our being. This means we have more emotional tone, depth, and capacity to work with, give, and enrich ourselves and this world.

We have more energy to work with and utilize.

But for that, we must accept what is. Whatever it may be. It's okay. It's only right now. We can change our lives instantly when we choose it in our hearts. That is the literal and divine truth of our reality. That power is always in our hands, which means that power is in our hearts.

When we're finally ready to lose weight.

When we're finally ready to stop drinking.

When we're finally ready to stop addictions.

When we're finally ready to stop playing games.

Figuratively or literally.

When we're finally ready to change our life.

When we're finally ready to be happy.

Whatever it is.

First, we accept who and where we are.

What we may and may not have done.
And all the emotions that come. All of it.

If we accept it, we can release it regardless of how hard it may be. Then comes the greater wherewithal to be more emotionally and mentally present to what is and begin from a greater depth and clarity within.

Sometimes, we may be able to; sometimes, we may not. As we bring in greater compassion for self, kindness toward self, and loving of oneself the best we can, it helps us to be able to accept the things we can and cannot change and breathe. Just breathe.

Self-compassion grows empathy, awareness, understanding, and even greater and deeper compassion and care for self. It gives you the space to breathe through the things that cripple us, for it opens your heart.

This is the subtle energy of attention and focused attention.

It's subtle. However, that shift is all it takes to birth a new reality.

It is always this subtle - everything.

Acceptance is the invitation to all of it.

Peace with Self and What is

One of the most challenging things is to make peace with ourselves and what is.

So now, acceptance is going well, or at least well enough. It's something you can do, or you're working on. It can still be a struggle sometimes, but at least we continue trying. That is all anyone can do and offer in life—their best, which is their heart. In truth, we all are doing the best we can. If we knew better, we would do better. That goes for anyone and everyone you ever come to meet. What more can a human being do? If we earnestly try, all the gifts meant for us come in time, for your energy always calls out to the Heavens and yourself!

And for the latter, for those that do not try as much, it seems that time also serves. Whatever folly we have lived through or been a part of or contributed to, how no event is ever wasted, and how all events in our lives serve for our highest and greatest good and unfold into life ever after. So, regardless of where we may be with ourselves and our relationship with ourselves, it's okay. No matter what it is, it's okay. It's okay whether this is yourself or someone you know, for there is grace in everything.

For love can be born and reborn any time of any given day on any given moment, simply in a divine instant like the phoenix rising from the ashes of all that has been to become the more of all it truly is, just as all that you truly are dearest. That is the journey—the birth of our heart and soul in this time and space reality.

But goodness, making peace with it. That is undoubtedly a whole new level of acceptance. Yes. It's certainly an ebb and flow. An emotional rollercoaster ride. Yes, it can be for sure, for you are releasing old patterns and ways of being conscious and unconscious.

Making peace with things releases the unease around the situation. It creates ease even more so and on a greater level than acceptance. It creates more ease around the situation, which means more ease in our emotional body, more ease in our feeling body, and more ease to release into the ethers. In a way, it is surrender—surrendering to what is on a deeper level than acceptance. There is more freedom of mobility here, both inward and outward.

But how is that possible, you ask?

It is seeing things from a higher perspective. Learning to look for the golden nuggets that will give you the grace to choose faith over anything else, or anything less than, and not let it harden your heart as it can for so many of us. That is the truest reality. That is peace. As we breathe through this while maintaining an open heart, it makes those spiky edges less so and even more rounded that you no longer feel the pain as you live your life, even as you move around. It may bump around as a volleyball in your being every so often or once in a blue, but your surrender and inner work lessen the hate and ache. The hate or ache you once had or any less than emotion around the situation, for you see the grace it has honestly released and provided within.

What is that grace, you ask? Yes, it can be so many things. Innumerable.

But it is more awareness of self, the truth of self, and the depth of self that one may never have ever begun to experience nor reach if not realized without this event.

The experience affects both within or without one's inner world and outer world, hence the greater love and deeper appreciation for self, thus the opening to self. Which also means greater love and a deeper appreciation for others as well. For some of us, for all mankind. Actual suffering opens the heart to no end, and a heart of genuine compassion is born within. Indeed, developing this knowingness and understanding deep within your heart versus your mind, how we are in every way on this journey called life and living together hand in hand and heart to heart.

And how sacred all life is. Every person's life.

It doesn't matter if you know the person or not; it doesn't matter. None of it does. What connects us is our humanity and our heart.

And with this knowingness, it brings you further into your heart, even more so. The nuance, level, and quality take on a more heightened depth and almost indescribable tone. Still, it is something one only feels and appreciates greatly once you're there. Entertainment and the media try to capture grace, but seeing it, reading about it, and then living it in your life as it unfolds within your heart is vastly different.

The difference is night and day. Everyone seeks this kind of magic, which can only be found within. Lastly, I mentioned actual suffering opens the heart. Yes, it can. We need not learn and grow in suffering. We can learn and grow in joy, too. That is also the beauty and the grace of what is. It's if we choose. All life is a choice. Once we tap into that knowingness, we can let so many things go. Peace and acceptance flow more freely because you have freed yourself within.

So, to recap.

Acceptance lets you manage processes and soothe your emotions.

Peace lets you accept, heal, and release your emotions.

Love of Self and What is

One of the most challenging things is to love ourselves and all that is.

But at the same time, it should always be easy to love ourselves and be love itself. That is who we are at our core and with every fiber of our being. This is so. Deep down, deeper yet still, in the depths of our being, we all know this as a fundamental and higher-knowing truth. The deep and abiding goodness within each person and all mankind and the true journey we are on, individually, collectively, and eternally.

When we love, it is unconditional acceptance, a genuine, wholesome appreciation, complete surrender, and true knowingness. It is true freedom and bliss. To dissolve all that binds until nothing holds you down but your love that always lifts and guides.

That is the power of love. Love is multiform, multipurpose, multidimensional, and multi-everything. One act of and from love has profound implications and ramifications for you, others, and humanity. We don't think of it or see it that way because we only focus on what's right in front of us. Still, if we took a bird's eye view, an angel's eye view, Heaven's eye view, the view of all eternity, or the divine view, we would see how true this is in size, scope, depth, and magnitude.

That is why love is the one enduring thing all humanity speaks of throughout the ages. It's not war, famine, or disaster. However, we speak of those things too. It is love above all. It is always about love. It will forever be about love. Our entertainment, music, songs, stories, and words are filled and fueled by love.

For who doesn't need reminding and remembering? It is the eternal story beyond and above all stories. It is THE story. It is the only story that moves us enough to open our hearts to the deeper truth and reality and touch upon a higher knowing that's simply waiting. It's the only thing that inspires us. It's the only thing we have any interest in. The only thing that moves us. No matter what story, movie, or situation, it's always about the human spirit and overcoming the deepest of challenges. It's a remembrance of the truth of who we are. For that is our journey.

It is both the answer and the question of humanity's lifetime for all time. It is our hope, guidance, and faith as we enact our faith and realize love on this day, within and without.

Our eternal eternity comes with every breath that takes us to grace, simply home to our heart.

Thereby birthing more beauty into this world.

Through acceptance, then making and creating peace with self and what is, the last step is to love what is. Then let that love grow to consume you whole until it becomes unconditional love birthed in your body, mind, heart, and soul until you are no more simply consumed in the fire of the depth of love itself. You've melted into Heaven, and Heaven has melted into you. Who is who, and what is what? You don't even know anymore. Yes, when it's that good, you don't know anymore.

Does it even matter? No. Your dreams have come true. You are true love. Yes. You are love true. Just as you are, in every way you are, you are—nothing more and nothing less.

You didn't need to be anything or anyone else. You didn't need to be a certain way. The only thing you had to do, if at all, was to be you in whatever that meant for you. Even that, too, can change as we change and evolve into the more of who we are. That is glory and grace, simply the power to choose what we choose and bring into our lives. Our entire life is about choice.

So then, speaking of choice.

Who will do the difficult thing?

And forgive all that you hate.

How do you love what you hate the most? With others, or various events in our lives, recent or long past, and yourself? No matter how much pain one endures or carries and where it came from, it's always about learning to love, forgive ourselves, and accept ourselves. That is the work. As counterintuitive as it is, as we do our inner healing work, we naturally work through those emotions. As we come to see, process, release old patterns of behavior, and strengthen what needs strengthening, we gently level up in every way.

All our anger and resentment or whatever less than emotion it may be toward another or an event as we work through it, after forgiving and releasing the external, the last part is always about forgiving and releasing yourself into this grace, too, regardless of if you had a part to play in what gives you turmoil, heartache, and heartbreak. The last step is always about forgiving and loving oneself unconditionally regardless of whether we did or did not have anything to do with it.

To release any remnants of anger, resentment, bitterness, hate, simply all victimhood. You are never a victim; no matter what happens, you are never a victim. You can align with higher knowingness and the knowingness of your spirit and call forth the strength and the guidance to see anew and chart a new path forward, a new way to release all that is less than. Just like that, you give it all up. You surrender and release with grace and ever-loving faith, and peace ensues gently. Love ensues. Freedom ensues.

You release yourself from yourself and all the ties that bind you through love.

And now you approach yourself and life in a more integrated and balanced way. From a place with more acceptance, peace, and the power to breathe and be, where the depth of love can root, bloom, seed, and grow even more so, and release from the depth of our soul and push vibrantly forth. From that place, it becomes clear how things had to be.

How each played a part and a role. The higher perspective is, maybe, deeper than the horrible people or horrible situation that caused such grief; perhaps that was their role to play in your life, ultimately to take you higher into a profound new sense of self that you otherwise would never have achieved by yourself and on your own. That, and how you had the strength to endure what you did and yet still see a way through the chaos and the pain. Yet, still hold onto your love, while many do not. Yes. Simply all of the above. Yes. All of the above. Is that not grace?

As we allow ourselves to come to the place of deeper compassion for ourselves, our hearts open even more. Then we begin to see the grace of all that is and what was and what forever shall be. The open, endless possibility called life and living, and most of all you.

Love is an unconditional acceptance, release, healing, and understanding of how everything serves and the complete and overwhelming gratitude that washes over your body, mind, heart, and soul. It's the complete transformation of one's being as the light softly pierces and radiates every part of your being. As we continue to visit this place, learn from it, and align with it, it's transformational every time, for it's the return of love itself.

That is the power of love, self-love, and unconditional love.

All that is less than dissolves.

For it simply has no place to hold.

It must cede and concede.

And all that's left is what simply is.

And that is, forever, the light.

You are of the light, my sweet.

You are of the brave, my love.

You are a symbol of peace.

You are the one.

You are love.

The Forever Journey of Awakening

True Compassion for Self

This is about deepening our understanding of compassion, for you realize now true self-compassion is proper self-care. This allows oneself to maintain, dive deeper, and align with oneself, further strengthening, expanding, and simply lightening all aspects of one's being. This allows you to be in the fullness of the meaning. To be, and be you, true and true, and that takes love.

Every major faith and religion talks about love. Meditation is a key component to help quiet the mind, but it's always about returning to the heart. That is the journey. We use fancy words, but it's that simple when we boil it down.

The idea of embracing love and who you are is so profound that there is no end to this. It continues to get deeper and deeper as you grow, no matter what age and the stage of the game you may be in.

So now, it's the real understanding and realization of ultimately owning that you are who you are and owning it, whatever your vibrational identity is. Once you do that, it hones it. It becomes you, and you become it. The freedom to truly explore and release it. Anything and everything.

And to feel and enjoy this and the reality of this truth as it expresses itself within your being and, hence, your life. To honor one's love and be it. To honor one's joy and to give it. To take time for ourselves should we need it, to realign ourselves back to this knowingness of the truth of who we are through greater self-compassion. That is how the journey continues forever.

Even at this stage, life will always arise. What great practice it is, too. For now, we get to truly hone everything we learned to every degree and subtle note in all the ways it applies to all the events in our lives.

Yes. There is no situation in life where love does not apply. It is always one facet or form. No matter what it is, it's always about the heart and comes back to the heart. At any and every stage. From the beginning to the end. It's just a different level and nuance each time.

To be rich in consciousness in all that you do.

Owning who you are means owning all that you know about love.

Not getting caught up, remembering your strength, and owning your light.

Practicing the truths of the masters who have come before.

Owning who you are and being it.

Staying away from the critical side.

Truly honoring self and loving self.

And appreciate self.

And all that you have.

And all that you are.

And the next time you think of something bad, you do not focus; direct your energy there and dwell. Or when someone comes to you with the horrible news of how everything is terrible in their lives, listen to them with an open heart and all your wisdom, but at the same time, understand there is greater grace at play and see the light that shines in their heart and their eyes.

Yes. It may have been a challenging event and story. It was what it was. You lived and came to all sorts of realizations and mostly realizations about self that will be endless, valued, and cherished for a lifetime. That will take you to places beyond everything and anything you can imagine and take you to the heights of ecstasy of being and beyond. The very thing, the very thing everyone is searching for-themselves. That is priceless, timeless, ageless, and neither cannot be bought or sold, nor can it be taught per se. It can only be lived and earned in a sense. By the opening of your heart. The offering of your heart. The awakening of one's heart.

So, in everything, in all things, there is no victimhood. That is true strength. That is holding onto the light. That alone will bring you further into your light. Then, the true acceptance, even more so, of all things, all events, all people, all situations, anything, and everything. How we all have our path and our time for things. That is all.

At this stage, you are, and that requires true self-care, which means true compassion and a deeper understanding and honoring of your love to be your love.

Holding the Energy, Holding Your Love

You have done your inner work and raised your mental and emotional well-being, the vibration of your being. That's what happens when you choose peace and love, and you choose you.

By now, you have witnessed miracles upon miracles that astound your mind even to this day. The true reality is that things of that nature are almost everyday occurrences. For a miracle of any size opens the heart wide. Or maybe because your heart is so open, you begin to see life for what it truly is, the miracle it is. That is how every day becomes a true, total, and complete gift where you feel this truth and this knowing deep within your very bones.

This gratitude and this knowingness fills your heart, for you hold the spiritual principles deeper than your mind, but in your heart. It's something you live and something you are, not something you conceptualize and intellectualize. This goes beyond mindset but into your heart. It's who you are. Love cannot be put in a box, and neither can you. You honor your love, hold your love, and continue to let love flow within your being, for you are love. You are true love.

This is how everything manifests and amplifies even more so through purity of spirit and being. This is pure alignment at its core and releases all the gifts in store. Both within and without, for love must attract love. It is the way of things.

Your eyes come alive, and they glow. Your heart is pure and flows. You can't describe it or explain it. Still, you know it's a different nuance to being when things become effortless and wondrous, and you ponder to yourself. Hmm. This is how it's meant to be; you hear a deep yes somewhere inside. Yes, it is.

You hold true to your principles.

You hold true to your core.

You hold true to you.

You hold true to love.

Because of this, all is given to you.

Being and Giving Your Love

It's time to be and give our love. Yes. At this point, or any point. Especially now, you are connected to your source, you are connected to your heart, and you feel it glowing in your very being.

Is it purpose, passion, or simply following our joy? It's all of the above. It's time to honor our love.

Some may have a calling or a passion to pursue. Some may have a desire or hobby they enjoy, and some may stumble upon trying new things. Whatever it is. Life did not change so much, but you did. Now, whatever you do and wherever you are, you will show up, do you, and give you, be the light true.

You allow the light to guide you. It's about living now. Even more so. To be so filled with love and life that it's now time to enjoy life and do what your heart sets out to do. Whether that means being a painter, cartoonist, playwright, architect, engineer, data scientist, entrepreneur, singer, or whatever it is.

Or even simpler, doing simple, meaningful things for you. It doesn't have to be big, like 'saving the world.' First, you already did that with your love. That alone is the gift. It's about what fills and fulfills you at your core. Now, you allow yourself to go there and do it while savoring every scrumptious moment. Be it gardening, knitting, sewing, biking, anything and everything. That is it.

It is now time to live.

And give your love.

And follow the love of your soul.

And offer it to the world.

Your world or the world at large.

Or even simpler,

The world of your heart.

It's one and the same.

For we are all connected.

By our one true name.

The sacred name of love.

And when there is more love and joy anywhere.

There is more love and joy everywhere.

You are now a part of this love that moves humanity forward.

Namaste.

You are a Master

What is a master? It is one who gets up again and embraces their life. Whatever that may mean, and rises to the joy of their task. More than the challenge, the joy of their life, and simply live it true and be you. That is a master, true and true. The truest journey of a lifetime. To be happy.

You do not see what is impossible. You see what is possible and true and good in your heart and life. You see the higher knowingness and let it guide and soothe your way. You keep faith no matter what happens. You honor all life as your own. You honor you.

Yes. You are a master, it's true.

The Result - You are Love Unleashed in Forever Bloom

The Forever Flow of the Heart and Soul

Flow is a timeless quality.

Everyone is all about business this and business that or hiding behind one professional title, label, or another. While all those things are important and needed, if not necessary, nothing beats true connection and aliveness to self and soul, which then translates to and into every area of your life. You are not your title; you are.

When you've found the reason, the purpose, your place within and without, there are no more questions; there is and only being. From pure being comes pure, inspired action. That is called alignment.

It's only in the being aspect from which all else stems—the flow of one's soul. Flow is a timeless quality, marked by boundless energy and an open heart and soul. How else is it supposed to flow?

This is you now. You don't need to read a book on flow. You just are.

Peace and Passion of the Heart and Soul

The fire of one's spirit.

The true coming alive is when you feel the fire burn you alive. It may or may not be a passion or a purpose for a specific cause, but the passion for life and living burns in your heart and soul. That is your purpose. To live. Because you understand what a precious gift this life is, no matter what it is, it is a profound gift that moves you to tears.

However, you could not feel this fire without peace. There is a calm, quiet strength that emanates from your being. That is the result of your continued inner work and faith. Raising your vibration every day. Simply doing the work, but more than work. It's not work. You just wanted to live in peace and know what that means. It was that simple. Nothing profound, but the desire to live and not be in pain anymore. That is what began this journey in the first place.

As we remove layers upon layer, you drop down to the level of being. Which only continues to get deeper as we live, but the peace and passion of the soul is undeniable. The fire and the calm. This is you now. You are one.

Joy in Your Heart and Soul

You allowed yourself to be yourself.

What you have done is take full ownership of your life. When you know you are in complete control, you wake up, act, and choose the things you wish to bring into your life from that place.

So, thereby, as you continue to do your inner work, hold love in your heart, and choose the loving way, the more love grows within you as you, for it takes true strength to journey upon one's being. It took the strength of heart and the power of love.

That power allowed you to change everything in your favor, even you. It seems like an impossible ask, but in reality, not so impossible at all. It is an inevitability and an eventuality for anyone who chooses this, for you stand in the power of your light. Yes, more power, the power of the truth of who you are at your core, which also means more joy in one's heart. True power is not force or strength but strength of heart and character.

How can one not be happy when you're in your heart? How can one not simply be filled and fueled by such intense levels of overwhelming, all-consuming gratitude to be here now? To finally say this, mean it, and know it to be true. The joy of utter gratitude for having come so far within ourselves to allow ourselves to be ourselves, whatever that may mean. This is the opening of the bud, the flower of your consciousness, and that is the journey of the heart. The journey of all humanity. The journey of love as it defines and refines itself as who you choose to be in the here and now, in this beloved eternity. Oh, the sweet serenity!

This is pure, unbridled joy. Not for any reason, but simply because you just are. If that isn't the best reason, I don't know what is. To be happy for no reason is an excellent and valid reason we should all adopt. For joy and laughter lightens the heart and soul and fills it so.

You have raised your vibration to a degree; this is just you now. It's not that you're super happy all the time, fake, or playing a role in any manner. Still, there is so much to be happy about and grateful about, simply all the sheer beauty in and of this world. It's tough to deny and ignore what simply is like you once perhaps did - not anymore! And you never will again.

Life is a source of joy.

You are your source of joy.

Love has the power to open doors.

Joy has the power to open hearts and souls, too.

This is you.

The world has opened, for you have opened.

You have opened to the world of your heart and soul.

You have opened to the great oceans of love beyond.

The great oceans of love within.

The great oceans of love without.

The great oceans, seas, and tides of all Heaven and Earth.

Let's sink into this love and melt away.

Honor this love and then give it away.

For what we give returns a thousand-fold.

This is how love never grows old.

This is the joy of your soul.

Welcome back home.

Desire to Give and More from the Very Depth of Your Core

Walking through the fires of one's demons in self and life is the most courageous and humbling thing one may ever do, for it is the true burning alive. Burning away all that is less than and burning awake all that is true, good, and beautiful in self and life.

Suppose one has suffered in life, as do we all. No one has the corner market on suffering. If one has truly endured great and unbearable hardship to the point of breaking, facing, and overcoming this pain. That is a profound human being. It's not about comparing our pain. Pain is pain. That is universal, as is love. To face such pain that is true strength indeed. True heart, indeed. True love, indeed.

It takes all you have and then some. Yet, through this process, we unearth our diamond—the diamond of our soul. You have the heart of true compassion. That gives you soul strength, soul power, a kind of fire one can't even describe, but you know it when you know it. You feel it when you feel it. Someone who has finally come alive. That's what happens when we face our deepest pain and then our deepest love. It's time to give it all away with all your love.

Whatever you may be called to do, you have birthed a true heart of compassion. No longer is the suffering you once endured a painful memory, but knowing how even something like that served you, too.

To be you now.

A person you love and respect.

The person you always wanted to be.

A free person.

With the fire of their soul awake and alive.

With the peace and passion that gently guides.

A pure desire to serve the whole.

Alleviate the pain you endured.

It is this that brings you joy.

Among many other joys.

And when it's that deep.

It must. It must. It must.

Come to be.

For it all already is.

For you are love unleashed.

Welcome back home.

CHAPTER FOUR

Markers of Note

"What lies behind us and what lies before us are tiny matters compared to what lies within us." — Ralph Waldo Emerson

Pendulum Effect

When we're beginning or in the middle of it or any time, but especially in the beginning when everything is so new, the idea of honoring our love, doing our inner work, and holding to the ideals of living in peace comes to you and captivates you so. It begins a whole new journey, a profound journey one can't begin to express.

As life is as life does, life happens for us all, and hiccups arise that may detract, demotivate, and demoralize you on your path. It knocks you off balance as you live through anxiety, turmoil, and internal unrest. The kind of emotional downturn that brings about a heaviness within us for days, if not weeks to months even. Then, sadly for some of us, even years to a lifetime.

Has that ever happened to you? When you're so emotionally hurt or taken that you can't get out of that funk for what seems forever and for however long it takes, every day is filled with dread and gloom, even if nothing is happening. The proverbial dark cloud over our heads, as they say. First, that is the power of our untrained mind.

Second, as we do our inner work and work through these emotions and events, we regain our internal composure and come back to balance over time. Just think of a pendulum. When you are at rest, the swinging ball is at center. Every time something happens, the ball starts swaying, and momentum and gravity take over and keep it going, and back and forth it goes. Eventually, it returns to the center over time, for it must!

Likewise, no matter how far and how wide our pendulum swings with all the frantic upsets we go through, as we do our inner work, we always come back to the center, too.

Yet, with each precious event, we learn more about others and, more importantly, ourselves. They say time heals all things. It certainly does help. Also, we learn how to balance and manage our energy with those of varied and different energy than you. Every person you meet is operating from a different vibrational tone level and degree.

Over time, that pendulum still swings, but we return to the center faster, quicker, or better each time. First, it swings high, low, and wide; oh, so wide! It sure does. However, within a reasonable time, within divine time, within the right time, the distance between the ball's swing and center lessens with each pass. That is the effect of your inner work and growth and, hence, your ability to manage all the challenges in your life.

It's not that things won't happen or that you are so accomplished, all-knowing, and all-seeing that you can escape challenges now. It's more so you've grown your internal level, knowingness, and ability to manage what may come with a deeper, higher, more grounded sense of self, in a sense, with the more of you. Hence, naturally, as we raise our vibration, things hold on less and less, the time decreases less and less, and things affect you less and less. You process it out of your system faster. The pendulum doesn't swing for long, not as long as it used to. You come back to the center faster.

You didn't lose a few months in the process like you used to, which means more time to appreciate and enjoy the precious gift called life we have been given. As you grow in your journey, you will see the miraculous healing effect of the inner work you gave to this endeavor and every event in your life. You know you are on your way when you notice things shifting faster for you.

So, take heart! Keep faith!

It's moments like these where we grow spiritual ab muscles of steel.

For it is moments like these that are too precious to name.

You will see, in time, how it all serves the sublime.

The greatest unfolding of yourself is divine!

Release Attachment to the Idea of Getting to that "High"

If, on your journey, you experienced that moment of awareness like I had, then you know what it's like. It may not be extreme, but any bit is still that potent and impactful and can profoundly change our lives and how we view and approach them, which triggers this process and journey.

How, for the first few years, if not for quite some time, you wish, and you wish, and you wish you could go back to that. To be in bliss again. To be at peace again. To be in grace again. The pain of that is pure torture. For how do we even begin to justify and rectify the reality of all that we lived through to the reality that is now. The reality that lives in our hearts, to the reality at present. This very reality that we know to be true with all that we are and every fiber of our being. How do we even begin to bring this about, let alone express it and explain it to anybody else?

It's also our attachment to that which keeps us in place. I'm not sure if that's something one can learn to let go of by reading but more so learn through living. Because in that sheer act alone, being with ourselves and experiencing ourselves, we learn to detach and be here now, no matter how beautiful any moment was. That is also the beauty and the grace of what is.

For you begin to see, even a moment of such magnitude filled with exquisite and unspeakable grace is equal to all everyday moments, even simply sitting in your local cafe and sipping on a cup of freshly brewed coffee. Yes. For if we are truly present in what is, that is the peace and the bliss that comes with and brings. That is the power of presence. Actual presence is a healing, a release, a complete and total awakening and enlivening, a regrounding to now, a regrounding to you, a regrounding to love itself, a regrounding to all life itself.

This is a reminder that we can gently strive toward releasing that attachment. The high is not the goal, no matter how much you want it or how good it is. That I understand; the high will soon come to the point where every day you breathe is just as sweet, dearest. That is in store if you stay true to your path and live. No longer will it be a high, but your everyday reality. That is the path of love. You begin to see with the eyes of love.

Living in the Present

When we are grounded in the now, many things are happening, even if not much is happening. First, your heart is just open. That alone is the gift. You are entirely in your body. You are fully in your flow. That is how we channel the divine into this world. The divine in you to come through in all that you do. Being present is the anchor from this world to the next, and your heart is the doorway with which it all connects.

This happens when you anchor the light, do your inner work, or even try to be a good person, aka listening to your heart. That is the payoff. You receive the priceless fruits of your heart's wish. You thought it was about living a good life and being a decent person, and it is, but what you receive is more immeasurable than what you give in return. When we honor our love, we receive love. We receive ourselves, our deeper selves, our true selves, our whole selves, and that only continues to grow forever in bloom, the beauty of you.

True presence is a reconnection to peace, bliss, healing, release, receiving, renewing, awakening, enlivening, ground, regrounding, you, love, life, all life itself, the more, the more beyond the more, and the more beyond even that. It is, in every sense, a true union of sorts. Of the purest kind. You. To be, and to be you, dearest. A true connection to self is also a connection to all that is.

Everything is about this: learning to be present. Present to ourselves. Which also means, to thy self be true. For if we are truly present to what is and what is within, or even simpler, if we only listen to our heart, then we can hear the inner calling that guides us to the direction of our greatest joy, our destiny that was foretold. The seed of the soul that desires to be and breathe in this time and space reality. For we all have a spark of the divine.

Yet that takes presence and being present to our emotions and ourselves. That is the journey. I honor you on your journey. For who will strive to be true. Except for those that do. You are the best of humanity. For this is the path of illumination. Even simpler, just joy! Life is meant to be fun. When you lighten up, you realize it's just time to live and have fun!

The power of one more present human being, one more person filled with love, one more person who is simply happy from their core, has the potential to irrevocably change the direction of all mankind and birth the kind of miracles the world has never seen before.

For that is the power of your heart and soul.

That is the power of love.

Physical

Often, when we are vibrationally leveling up or, in other words, doing our inner work, learning to listen to our heart, and working on ourselves, over some time, you can see the dramatic change of energy work through our physical body for everything reflects the energy we hold within.

Our face lightens up. You no longer carry that same furrowed brow and heaviness in your eyes. You slowly stop shifting your eyes all the time in fear and worry. You lower the eyes of suspicion and begin to carry the eyes of appreciation. The tension in your shoulders and your back relaxes, and your gait changes from scurrying to enjoying and appreciating what the day brings. Yes, even just the muscles in our body relax, and we may carry ourselves differently. The tone of voice may strengthen with presence where, as prior, it was quite low and meek. There may even be a joyous glow and flow about you.

Often, healers of any modality will begin to see the subtle shifts in their clients. It's the natural process as unconscious energy becomes free and lightens your being.

It's like getting a facelift, but a soul lift, and hence a physical lift. Just look at those so unhappy about their lives and dread each day. It's all over their demeanor, their attitude, and their life.

Just look at someone harboring great resentment or any less than emotion in their being. That energy builds and compounds over time; you can see, sense, and feel it in a person's being. It's in their tone, in their speech, in how they approach things, in how they address things, in how they live their life, and in how they operate their life. It's in everything.

Or, when a person has felt regret for an extended time and finally found forgiveness and redemption, they feel a burst of energy and feel free to live again. It's like a heavy weight has been lifted from their being, and in a sense, it has! The energy of any less than emotion is always that heavy and weighs the body down. You just come alive when you release that and the soul is free. You can usually notice it in someone or yourself. For everything is energy and a reflection of one's energy.

We all have gut instincts on various life matters and those we meet. Is this person trustworthy? Do I like them? Do I not? Or does this feel right to me? It's all based on energy, the energy we carry, and the energy we give.

Everything is energy, and energy is stored in our body.

Mental

As we gradually learn to tame the mind, the mind comes in service to our spirit, and no longer is it the master of our fate. As we continue to do our inner work, it is possible to have it simply stop one day. All the noises and chitter chatter. It can stop. I mean, it's as simple as that. It just stops. It stops working against and fighting against you but becomes a quiet place and a source, if not a resource, of and for your greatest champion and cheerleader.

As we live and grow in this life, in the beginning, all we hear and all we know is the constant mind chatter of how you're not good enough, how you can't do that, or how it's not possible for you, and that's putting it mildly. In our mind, we all let go and say it all, and not very nicely, I might add. This can be difficult, and for those of us who say you don't speak that in your mind, if you vibrationally feel it, if it's on vibrational repeat in your emotional body regularly, it's the same thing.

On top of that, we all have busy lives, whether it be school, work, or family. Juggling so much at once or not, the mind can take you down and leave you feeling completely drained, and you have no idea why. It's because all our energy is tied up as we let our thoughts and emotions sway us to their will. That's what happens when we constantly repeat the same story; we tell ourselves over and over again, whether consciously or unconsciously. Like a dandelion blown across the winds, our energy is spent and scattered with all the negative mental chatter as it closes our eyes to the truth of what it is.

Mental detoxes are great for this. Quieting the mind helps, but no one can meditate 24 hours a day for 365 days straight unless you do. However, most of us have lives to live and things to do. Although on one level, true presence is in itself a waking meditation. Holding love in our hearts also has the same effect.

Lastly, an important note is that daily meditation grows conscious awareness and creates the space between the chatter for the silent awareness to arise. For most of us, it's a slow and gradual process; for the few, it can be instantaneous. Rare, but it can happen. Much like the apple falling on Newton's head as he discovered the law of gravity or Einstein's famous Eureka moment as he discovered the relationship between energy and mass, otherwise known as $E=mc^2$, or even simply as Buddha sat by the bodhi tree that fateful day that changed his life forever. The rest is history, as they say.

Insight comes when it comes. It comes in varying degrees to the level of our allowing and receiving, but when it comes, it certainly does come.

Yet that aside, so then, what do we do? A mental detox. You commit to just feeling good and not indulging in any negative thoughts in your mind that may arise telling you how ugly, stupid, dumb, fat, skinny, whatever less than statement that comes up for you toward yourself or others. We commit to just not going there and seeing what happens. It may take a month or a bit longer. Still, I promise, if you do it within time, it will stop, or at the very least, you will see noticeable improvements, drastically assisting you in the journey of your being. The benefits will reflect in your life because it's an energetic response to an energetic release.

Without the label of mental detox, it simply means committing to your truth, your heart, and your love. It's the level of integrity and standards we hold for ourselves and the caliber we wish to hold for ourselves in our being. That's all it ever is. So, it goes beyond a short-term detox to an ingrained habit and integrated way of being. Of course, being human, we all forget from time to time, but this is what it is and why it's so powerful. It takes care of itself on every front and every level if we hold. Hold true to love. Yes, if we act by and through love.

And the day will come; it's like WOW! I'll never forget the day I experienced a tranquil, calm, and nurturing stillness in my mind, aside from that initial time that started it all. I committed, and I don't even know for how long, but I decided to do so. Then, one night, while driving home from work, for the first time I didn't hear you're so stupid or any less than thought, emotion, or anxiety arise within me. It was silent for once, and then a deeper silence washed over me. It blew my mind to the point I got shivers up and down my body because the stark contrast between before and after was unbelievable, especially when the less-than mental chatter had been practiced for so long, consciously and unconsciously. This left a tangible yet undefinable field of spaciousness, which was also unbelievable. Then, slowly, I heard a different voice. It's all right, you're okay, you got this. I was mind-blown, mind-blown all over again. This was truly surreal because it was foreign to me to experience kindness and warmth from myself, and yet, oh, how soothing it was to have a friend.

So yes, to mental detoxes! You don't have to tell anyone. Just do it. It can be a fun game you play with yourself and see what happens. What do you have to lose except everything to gain?

Over time, things may arise, upsets and more, upsets galore, but your mind is no longer at war with you in 24/7 complete annihilation mode. You can now work through things and process things with and from a better vantage point, from a place of loving kindness within, and if there is a hurdle, otherwise, for a much shorter duration. Either way, whatever it is, you are finally on your side now, for you are the master of your mind and not the other way around.

Emotional

Emotions are always a sign, an indicator of where we are within. Suppose we hold faith and try to emotionally work through, piecemeal, or detach from the chaos of our emotions. In that case, we begin to see that's all that it is, another data point and dataset of what's occurring within you.

Emotions are the greatest gift of life. To feel the depth of who we are and the depth of all life itself. To feel the wellspring, the overflowing, overwhelming, overarching depth of love within and without, is one of the greatest honors and joys. Still, it's about fine-tuning our emotional receptivity and sensing ability, raising our awareness and consciousness, and doing our inner work so we may begin to hear the depth of our being.

When anyone has struggled with any addiction, mental, emotional, or physical struggle, once you work through that and release that from your system, you realize how you used whatever it was to numb yourself to your emotions to avoid the pain. It helped you escape yourself and your reality instead of simply being here now. After you overcome something as tremendous as that, in whatever form it be for you, and everyone always has something, you realize you'll never do it again. You understand the dynamics of what led you there, how, and why. It begins from avoiding pain and presence and not having the higher information to learn how to process and be with it.

The greatest gift we've been given is to feel.

The most precious thing you can do is feel what you were avoiding, everything there is to feel, and more. For that is one of life's greatest pleasures and joys, to feel the beauty of everything, our humanity's beauty, our divinity's beauty, and the depth of it all as we live and breathe.

If we allow the feeling, then we are open; if we are open, then we are open to the more and all that brings both within and without.

What if what you are feeling is not beautiful? As long as we face the issue earnestly in our being, that intention alone holds the energy and the space for grace to show up and do what it does best: soothe, ease, guide, and release from within and or without. Along with that, the best part is continued energetic intention, aka the sincere intention of your heart, creates momentum for greater insights of wellbeing to come in and flow through.

Often, the answers may or may not come right away. As long as we spend some time within our being versus blatantly ignoring the situation and not taking any accountability responsibly or even just seeing what it is, that is all anyone needs to do for who doesn't want to solve the answers to their problems. We all do. When one is serious about addressing it or lives by and honors their heart, we naturally do this anyway. This is how guided we are from the start.

If some time has been given, or you're just not getting anywhere, or if it is that painful, shake it out and do something healing, soothing, or fun to release the energy. We always want to gently break negative energy patterns versus staying there too long and sometimes falling and sinking in.

As you continue this practice through the experience of various events in your life, you grow a deeper understanding of the power of facing yourself and feeling it all, no matter what happens. You begin to truly live with that integrity and the wisdom you have gained, that way of being. At the end or the beginning, nothing else will ever compare except to be fully present from now on out, not so much to make up for the time lost, but more so the time that is now found exquisitely. For now, this time for you is beyond sacred and precious but a true honor and a gift to live, which only heightens in full feeling, magnitude, and grace as we live and learn what it means to come alive and live life on our terms, by our standards, the standard of our precious sacred heart beating within the very bosom of being.

Emotions are our guidance system. Whatever it is and wherever you are, it's okay! Just another data point to ponder upon, is all! If we are love, and yes, we are, then feeling anything less than love, light, happy, and free shows us there is something to be curious about.

Yet with emotions, we all have a wide range of sensitivity, different things that we're sensitive to, and the depth of which we feel it all and more - or not. It always feels like a burden for everyone. Still, it may sometimes even feel like an overwhelming, debilitating hardship for the extra sensitive. To be so attuned to everything you can't detach. How daunting it can be to begin our journey and live in and from the heart if all we do is feel it all and more. It would be unbearable.

Many worldwide can relate to this and who hasn't felt that way before when things become too much, regardless of it all. I can say sensitivity is a strength, and that strength will carry you to the depths of Heaven itself and beyond.

There is truly grace here, as sensitivity is how it starts. That depth you feel, to feel every emotion in your being, and sensitivity to everything within and without is a skill. It is precisely that skill that will take you to where you want to go.

While the rest of the world has to learn discernment in this regard and sharpen and hone this way about them, this is something you already have. It's simply a matter of refining and attuning; energetic tweaking is all. That is it. No matter who we are and where we are, sensitive or not, this is it for us all.

As we learn to embrace this, work through this, and understand our emotions and emotional sensitivity, we begin to realize it is not a curse but the truest blessing, if not the greatest gift; you will, in time, also see the gifts therein lie for you. The blessing called life, your life, your love, and love itself is simply here for you.

That you even get to live and be alive and give the very depth of your love, the depth of your joy, the depth of your being. It is only such that would fulfill you, and naturally so for being sensitive to one's light, being, and internal world is how it starts.

The opening of the more and ever after.

The opening to ecstasy itself.

That concepts, such as bliss, are not merely written about in books.

But a tried-and-true reality for those that choose.

And it's all there and possible for you too.

All bliss and ecstasy are a pure alignment to self and soul.

Spiritual

We are truly spiritual beings living in this world. We often forget. Let alone how often are you surrounded by like-minded people who tell you yes, this is so. Beliefs aside, even simply, like-minded people who genuinely desire to live in their heart as a fundamental way of being with the true willingness to go within to face and feel it all. With that attitude or desire, there is a natural reverence for all life, our life, and the underlying precious sacred nature. There is a deep ingrained humility, appreciation, and grace for the delights of it all, no matter what it may be, with a natural resilience to perceive and receive all that is good, our greatest good, and the highest good for all.

For most of us or some of us, it depends upon our life path, which is usually not the case, and we are not surrounded by life-affirming people and situations. However, as we travel this inward journey, we begin to see the miracle that is you. The miracle of life is astounding, but the miracle you are is resounding, for there is none like you. I know this to be true. With all my heart, I know this to be true.

We are spiritual beings having a human experience. Intellectualizing this is one thing. Feeling it until it becomes a deep knowingness and visceral reality is another, for it radically changes the direction and dynamics of one's life, if not the very driving force. Let's feel this one, the very depth, truth, and the heart of it. Once we truly feel the core of anything deeply, it fully opens the doors one can only dream. This can mean many things, and yes, please let your imagination run wild. This is the stuff fairytales are made of. The word fairytales does not do justice to the reality of this glorious wonder and truth that is a part of our everyday lives, for it is mystical and magical in divine action and attraction. Oh, the satisfaction!

Everything in this life is born from spirit and energy. Our desires pull it through from one world to the next so that everyone may come to enjoy, appreciate, and share the beauty that one birthed, especially you!

That is the basis of the law of attraction and the spiritual nature of it. Everything is spirit; you are spirit; hence, as a spirit, you have the limitless source and power to draw into this time and space reality the deepest wishes of your being, whatever that may be and regardless of what it may be. It matters not what it is; if it's a sincere desire, that's as good as gold.

Speaking of gold, sometimes we get caught up in the material world, thinking it's bad or good or placing one label on it or another, but regardless of the matter, everything was born from spirit. You have the same ability to create all your heart's desires to your heart's content. The material world is not bad or wrong. Our attachment to it and the meaning we give it determines its value. However, if there is inherently no story, then everything is.

You are a powerful creator, so let's appreciate everyone's manifestation and think about everything you want to manifest! This is your world, too, and you get to choose and pick everything in your reality down to every nut and bolt.

You are a beautiful spirit.

Let us honor our spirit.

Energy

Where energy goes, focus flows, and everything expands from that place. It makes you wonder what energy I am operating from, what energy I am offering, what energy I am growing within my being because that is what we are not only giving but living into.

In a sense, this is what you call karma. We already live in the energy we hold within our being, which creates the thoughts, actions, and attracting power to make it a reality. Whatever we attract is always filled with the subtle yet oh-so-powerful lessons that, once learned, release and dissolve that karma. You no longer bring forward the same situations but create a new from a cleaner, more conscious place within.

It's as simple as that. Everything truly is energy, and when energy patterns are practiced long enough, they become ingrained and sometimes unconscious from our field of awareness and discerning. No need to fret, though; our life experience is an exhilarating opportunity to release, renew, and refine the truth of who we are.

Since everything is energy, on a basic level, your thoughts vibrate or hold a particular frequency, resonance, or energy. It's not a woo-woo thing; it's the energetic quality of the emotion you hold within your being, aka the amount of love we are allowing and holding or not.

You realize that conscious and unconscious behaviors are deeper than behaviors. Still, down to the slight emotions, one may feel within and how the energy of these emotions all play a part and add to the collective momentum of self and others. All we ever do is affect ourselves and each other with what's going on in our internal reality, creating a bigger manifestation of our shared reality. It almost feels like we are at the mercy of what happens and what life brings us, but that is not the case.

The power of our focused energy magnifies every thought and feeling. So do not give attention to that which does not deserve our attention. That takes practice and is similar to growing spiritual ab muscles of steel. Suppose you consciously realize the truth and sincerely desire to break negative patterns or break free. That intention will allow you to catch yourself better occasionally, slow down the unconscious patterns, and eventually release them.

Over time, you become better at catching subtle cues that indicate to you, oh, I'm doing it again, I'm indulging in a less-than thought, your chest is tight, your back is slumped, your face is red, or a mixture of reactions one may have. We always have ample clues to where we are because of how we feel mentally, emotionally, physically, spiritually, or even simpler, the quality of our joy. All this is how our energy is being used and directed at the time, and once we get conscious of it, we can get curious, readjust, and begin again. That is the very definition and basis of what we call a miracle.

All life is energy, and now you are the true magician of this world and the next. You are a magnificent being who can harness your energy and create what you will by the power of your intention and focus. You will focus and use your energy to serve your greater good, which means the greater whole.

For we are one.

And one we all are.

Synchronicity

There are always synchronicities in life. We are all a part of the whole that guides us all, no matter who we are, where we come from, or what we have or have not done. This is how divinely guided all humanity is. However, suppose we are truly embarking on the inward journey. In that case, synchronicities almost happen even more so, to much greater degrees and intensities. They are always happening, but now we have the wherewithal to see sense and recognize the uncanny nature of what is and what is occurring around us right before our eyes.

Yet isn't it always like that, though? How often is the answer to the question sitting right on the tips of our noses? When we're ready, we're finally ready to glance that way and begin to see what is there. Not just in this regard but in all regard. How everything is always right there for you all the time. It's only a matter of perspective, time, and divine time.

In the past, often, fortunate blessings would come out from the left field and unfold before your very eyes just when you needed them the most or not, ranging from the direst of situations to the fun, light, lucky surprises that tickle our being.

Yet despite even this, the great abundance being poured over you that seems to come out of nowhere, you just casually shrugged it off and called it a mere coincidence. You did not notice or take it all in, simply all the good in your life and savor its sweetness. The good things, good happenings, good events, good synchronicities, good blessings, right people, right time, right place. Simply all that is good, all the wonder and the grace, and the everyday miracles that take place in our lives from the big to the small.

We're so trained to look for what's wrong and what's bad often because our paychecks are tied to the level of problems we solve, so naturally, it makes sense to be proactive in this regard. Yet, have you noticed sometimes, if a strategy works in one area of our lives, we bring that same approach to all the other areas in our lives because how we do one thing is how we do all things? Then naturally, when our mindset is trained to see one way and one perspective, how can we ever begin to see what's there all along? Like all the miracles that are and the miracle that you truly are. For you are, you know. You are a miracle.

Yes. You are the greatest synchronicity in and of this world. All the factors that had to align to bring you forward. The sheer fact that you even exist is a statement in itself. The truth is miracles and synchronicities are more commonplace than you may think, than many may think. Only if we open our hearts does it all sparkle and blink like twinkling stars in Heaven's grand soap opera rink.

That's the thing: the mind only took anyone and everyone so far. It's always the heart that takes you all the way home. The heart that opens the door. The heart that calls for more. The heart that gives and brings guidance. The heart that speaks to you. The heart. The heart. The heart. It's the heart that releases it all. It's by and through the heart that we give. It's by and through the heart that we receive. It's by and through the heart that we even breathe.

So, the next time blessings or miracles happen, or bad or stressful things happen, at least do yourself a favor and try and look for the whole picture versus a small portion. Zoom out, imagine the bigger picture, and wonder what it may say. You may get an answer. To affirm the good and to see the good. Because it's there, that way, when you receive a blessing, when it becomes shown to you one way or another, either within or without, you can affirm and acknowledge it sincerely within. When hiccups happen, you can give yourself perspective, breathe, and make room for natural intelligence and the higher perspective to arise within. The world is not falling apart, and there is more to this than meets the eye, and it's all a matter of time.

Then, our entire life is synchronic, and the divine is at play. How everything is and how everything serves if we only let it and allow it into our lives and our hearts. Then, our life becomes our very art.

Soul Connections

Much has been said about soul connections. Whether it's fantasy, pure speculation, or has some significant merit and basis in reality, it's a fun idea to daydream about. It's what we've all done from time to time, dreaming about the love of our life, a love of some kind, or someone who will know us with but a single breath. Can a love like that exist? Does that happen in real life? What are all these magical love stories based on? Lastly, the most important question is how do I meet them?

The idea that there is someone out there, if not several special someones, that resonates with you on the level of your being is a fascinating concept that many romance novels try to capture and have run with. However, the truth is when one is truly on the journey of awakening or inner discovery or journey back to one's heart, aka you, things like this happen. Naturally, because you've developed your conscious awareness enough to know enough to honor one's heart, you are taking a different vibrational stance in life, and that is what you are attracting—your open heart.

On a basic level, when your heart is open, you are open to life, ourselves, and all the ideas your heart creates and then takes. Perhaps even open to all the ideas heaven guides and gives as they release inspiration's floodgates. Not only that, but you are happy to take them and make them. You are operating from a place of joy versus lack. Is it your higher self, or is it you? All great questions, but the heart is the heart, and that's all anyone ever needs to know.

Yet, on this journey, once in a while or occasionally, you meet a true kindred connection that is so uncanny it blows your mind away and takes you straight into your heart. The kind where, upon meeting someone, within some time if not immediately, you recognize a deeper consciousness, a recognition of some kind, where you instinctively know, understand, and feel who this person is, how they operate in the world and in themselves, their personality, their values, their sensitivity, their way of being, their heart, simply them.

When I say it takes you straight into your heart, it is not a trite statement or an overstatement. If anything, it may be an understatement because the true experience of the heart, let alone sharing that with someone, is something one never forgets. There are no words in life to articulate this profound beauty, the depth of which knows no bounds, hence the heights of which also knows no bounds, which ultimately means sheer unbridled joy and everything that comes with that.

You might experience uncontrollable laughter, giddiness, playfulness, and excitement. If you are a timid person, all that leaves you. If you are an overt and outward person, you experience stillness and presence. All parties experience openness and freedom. It melts all your defenses, and your heart opens like a flower. It has met a vibrational match in this life, and your bud has opened. The nutrients were a kindred soft love from both within and without, the recognition of a kindred soul.

That saying you don't know love until you find it. You don't know what you don't know until you know; that applies here. This is where it comes from. When the heart truly opens or is truly met on the level of the heart, there is tenderness, openness, sensitivity, surrender, kindness, excitement, and, above all, love. It is an experience; Every. Single. Time.

There is no specific number per se of soul connections one may have, but the more open we are with self, and depending upon life circumstances, things like this may happen more than once in a lifetime, if not several times, if not a few more after that. Ultimately, if we were to get technical, all humanity is a soul mate if we truly boil it down. For who is not love? We are all love.

Yet, for the truly rare soul connections, aside from the instinctual knowingness, you are bombarded with cues and signs from every level of your being. Some things may become viscerally apparent to you and open up your senses to such a degree you begin to see with a higher seeing in all the areas of your being. This can be left up to interpretation and one's imagination, which is how it should remain. For the intangible is intangible. It indeed can be and is a mystical, magical, wondrous experience.

You don't need to get to know someone. You already know who they are. As you get to know them, it affirms everything you already know. What a true gift and blessing this is. It means you are on your path. Naturally, like does attract like, and if open, we begin to meet people of a similar nature or vibration, or even simpler, a similar heart to one degree or another.

Of course, you should do your due diligence and get to know someone over time, but that is the gift. It is enjoyable to finally meet someone who touches you in your soul like no other person can. Then, it becomes about the heartfelt appreciation of another human being, regardless of it all. How sacred that is. How wondrous that is. How beautiful that is, and how blessed you both are.

Soul connections like this are rare; you never know when they'll come around. Still, each one is so different and unique in every way and matches you for who you are and where you are within your being at that moment in your life. It is a true resonance—the most remarkable, uncanny, wonderful, delightful, joyous resonance.

This is when all facades fade and fall away. Not that you had any, but connections of this kind automatically open your heart to such a degree you can't help but speak from that place, from the depth of your being, and share what's on your mind, even more, unfiltered than normal. Not only does it feel so natural, but you're shocked at yourself because you find you can't help yourself. The words spill out of you! Let alone you don't care because speaking with this person and spending time with them is so enjoyable, incomparable to any other friendship or person in your life; it is almost a sort of bliss. The experience of this breaks the mold of friendship, for these people already have the keys to your heart.

That is also what the power of presence does. It creates and offers a space for oneself and others to be and be as they are. That is a profound gift you offer in being alone because you did your inner work and could give it to yourself first. Even if growing one's conscious presence was something you were working on because you are so in your heart, it naturally comes about, for that is what the heart does.

You meet the most fascinating people on the journey of your being. Yet that happens when your heart and soul are in charge because that's the lens you view and operate from, the place you are attracted from, and the level of your being.

There are varying levels, degrees, and types of soul connections. As mentioned above, some strike you at your core, and then some share a resonance and familiarity to varying degrees. You meet people who are all called in different ways to different things in different areas of life.

You might share a specific passion, skill set, or joy. You might share the same vision of humanity or seeing the world. You might share the same values, depth, and sensitivities within one's being. You might share a similar calling, but it's hard to miss. Either way, God bless is all I have to say.

Some moments, if not all moments, are divine. This is one of them. When you meet those who are truly kindred of a kind. When people like this meet, it's a healing and a release for both parties involved, saying good job, you are on your way, and you are not alone in your endeavor and the endeavor of your life.

Despite this vital connection, we all have our paths and lessons in this life, and they are no different, as you are no different. Some meetings are for a brief time, a long time, or any time. What is that saying? People come into your life for a reason, a season, or a lifetime. Regardless of what it may be, it is irrespective of time, for this person will always stay with you and always be with you at the level of your heart. Seasons may change but love truly is eternal.

Mirror Effect

On a lighter degree, sometimes, once in a blue moon, you meet those who share an almost mirroring effect. They may or may not share similar values to the extent and degree of true soul connections. Still, you share remarkable similarities that are hard not to notice.

It can be an alignment of many factors at once, like having the same car, passions, dreams, and directions in life; it can be any number of things. One thing is for sure. You will undoubtedly notice.

It can be as silly and surprising as wearing a similar outfit to another person in a seminar halfway across the country several days in a row, and the only seat open in the class is next to this person. What are the chances, right? It was like life was asking us to meet and ensuring we did. Not only was the seat open, but we dressed alike too. In the entire room, we looked like twins for several days in a row. The list of uncanny coincidences goes on and on. When amusing things like this happen, it's hard not to strike up a conversation when it's so glaringly obvious that you begin to say, "Oh wow, okay!" You say hi and laugh!

After some time, all you can do is smile on your journey. Initially, it might be affirming and magical. It will always be, but now, you smile and appreciate life's great mystery and joy and simply being open to it all.

All Relationships are Divine

Relationships elate our being to such heights for it is the true expansion of the heart. Yet, I know relationships can also be our greatest source of pain, whether that be that of family, friends, partners, coworkers, acquaintances, or anyone else—even the relationship with self.

Beyond all this, though, with all the kinds and types of people one encounters, all relationships are divine. Yes. All relationships are sacred and divine, for each brings a purpose. It doesn't have to be a grand purpose or a mighty purpose. Whenever you meet someone, you meet another soul, and that's saying a lot. Have you ever thought about that? Every person you meet is a living, breathing heart, just like you. You might have grown up differently with different circumstances, but who doesn't feel?

We are born into this world at different parts and times with different paths and lessons, with a different blueprint and purpose of and for our being, so what a blessing it all is that it simply even is. When so many of us run on autopilot, what a true miracle it is to feel at all and meet on the level of the heart.

Yes, what a true honor it is to meet those you meet and connect with those you connect with and share a moment in any capacity, even if it's as simple as a pure smile. Love is always in the eyes, and everyone always feels that. A pure smile means a pure moment means pure presence. When you share a moment of pure presence, is that not always sacred and divine? How else does our light shine?

Every person is divine, has the divine's spark, and is connected in their own way. How we choose to honor ourselves, our hearts, and our light is another matter, but that is the journey. That is the journey we are all on.

What is deeply fascinating, though, is that each person comes into our life at the right time, showing us and teaching us, offering us a gift just in their natural way. The nature of this gift is to be determined, but whatever it is, it always takes us further into self and self-love if we allow it to. All life is a choice; we choose it all, even the experience and circumstance, consciously and unconsciously.

All relationships are divine, even the relationship with self. You are divine. Hence everything in this life is a reflection of the relationship we have with ourselves and takes us further into self. Hence, all life is divine. It will shine in due time, if it has not already, for Heaven is already yours.

That idea we are all walking each other home is more than an idea but the true reality of what is going on. Every blessed person you meet is an angel, even if they did not act accordingly, for there is divine grace in all things, meetings, and people. It's only if we're willing to open our eyes and hearts to see sense and know this to be true and, more importantly, how true it is for you and how it applies to your life.

Once you sink into that knowingness, the gifts are endless; the grace and gratitude are endless. Sometimes, the tears are endless, too. After that, the joy is even more endless, boundless, and ecstatic.

The Light Turns On

Then one day after some time, after years of doing your best to honor and live by your love and continuing to do your inner work and release all that arises regardless of what it may be, all that time you spent is not in vain nor is it a waste and has multifold benefits than just immediate, for with all that effort and the energy you poured and gave, one day, on that fateful day, the light turns on.

Yes. The light turns on, pouring onto you a thousand-fold and more.

You have grown enough now to have enough receptivity to see, sense, perceive, and receive. It's not so much about believing now but more so the understanding of the experience and the experience of understanding together.

That begins a whole new journey, a more profound one, a more prosperous one. The most satisfying journey. There are no words for this journey. The journey of you. The journey of love as you are and just as you are. Nothing more, nothing less.

There is a flow. There is a flow to all things. There is a flow to your life. There is a flow to the world. There is a flow to the universe. There is a flow, and we, too, are a part of this great flow. We are a part of that, and at the same time, we are that. We are all a divine expression of love in all its forms and faces.

Suppose you've begun the journey of awakening or, in other words, the journey of love, self-love, which leads to love for and of all things. In that case, that is the depth of love itself when unconditional love has been born within you. As the depth of love reignites the very fire of your heart and soul, your very life, and the very reason of and for your life. It's truly a renewal on all levels and all fronts. Simply in every way, a person can awaken.

Awakening to love is a forever journey. Constantly renewing, constantly expanding, and constantly evolving takes you to new heights within and without. The kind of heights that are so unspeakable, one can only bear witness to the grand grace that runs through every fiber of our being and the true beauty of this world, and it's true. The world is beautiful because beauty is now in your eyes, and beauty has been born within; you allowed yourself to rise above as you let your heart flourish like a beautiful white dove.

You are a beacon of light in this world.

This I know to be true.

As we walk our walk in this lifetime, we journey together.

I know sometimes one feels alone for whatever reason. It's okay. It's only right now. Everything is temporary. As is our life. Yet, our love and the truth of who we are is eternal. Our work in this lifetime is to embrace who we are, our joy.

Sometimes, there are bumps along the way that devastate you entirely to no end. Do not give up hope, and do not lose faith. Even in moments like that, when the ground beneath your feet is taken and shaken from you, there is grace in all things for all time. That is more than mere hyperbole. It's just the simple truth.

It's a matter of seeing the higher perspective, and everything dissolves. Everything truly dissolves. It dissolves the parts of you that needed release anyway. It gives you greater stores of energy to work with and utilize and revitalize with an even greater fervor. With that, a greater resolve, heart, and commitment to continue forth. Everything in this life unearths the more, the more of you, and then the more of all that is. Simply, the more.

Whatever your faith may be, we are a part of something greater, a greater whole. Physics itself boils everything down to atoms and energy, how we are simply a part of the cosmic soup—a blip of light in the expanse of all of time. However, long or short our time may be, we get to own our light and do with it what we will, our heart and soul dreams fulfilled.

As we walk this life, as we continue to keep the faith, do the best we can, be earnest, sincere, and open to what is. As we strive to do our inner work and live by the values of our heart, one day, that energy, all that work you gave and offered, through tears and love, pain and joy, it all compounds over time and grows until the dam breaks, and the flow turns on.

People always talk about the flow state, but this is deeper than feeling good or listening to a soft soundtrack and feeling peaceful. This is a flow unlike any other. It's the flow of all heaven and earth. It's the flow of your heart and soul. It's the flow united as one, together in you.

All your prayers. All your love. All your faith. It was like coming home to grace every time you plug into the outlet for renewal, regardless of whether the light was on. Every good deed, every loving thought, every loving choice is like this and this profound. Until one day, you plug in, the light finally turns on, and you feel a remarkable flow.

There's nothing one can say except something you feel. There is no doubt in your mind because with this comes even more heightened sensations and knowingness. Also, our natural gifts suddenly emerge and become even more apparent to you. The desire within you heightens. Everything heightens. The air is crisp. The air is clean. The air is beautiful. Life is beautiful. You do not have rosy-colored sun goggles. This is you. This is plain old you. Pure you. Breathing.

That's it.

You don't need to try to be happy. You are happy, and more than that. You are, and that's that. It's not about being happy always but reaching and releasing that inner joy that knows no bounds. With pure gratitude in our hearts, it's just inevitable.

Now begins a whole new journey. The journey to come alive even more so than ever before. To reach the heights of pure ecstasy. Ecstasy is another word when you are being totally and radically you. Bliss is synonymous with the truth of who you are. Pure alignment evokes bliss. Being true to you does this.

There will never be enough words to describe the joy you feel inside. Poets have penned and certainly try to describe the inexplicable love and depth of love that overrides and overrules our senses and our souls. Yes, in your love and the flow of your love, which is the gift you give yourself and the world, this is your grace, your honor, your life's work, and life's joy. Love, and to give your love.

It is only this that fulfills you now. Nothing else will do. Now, you have greater faith to follow through because of all the love you gave in the past as dues. Heaven has opened to you in your heart. It's true. For when you give love, one receives love. It is the way of things.

With this vibration and flow, things may open for you more naturally, so within your core, as we get settled into this new way of being, shedding more of all that no longer serves. That is always a continual renewal. As we awaken to the truth of who we are, every layer we reach removes another layer we didn't even know we had. It is that deep and that profound.

More than that, deeper than that, is the revitalizing of your truth and the truth of who you are! And naturally, all that no longer serves can no longer bind nor hold. All you have are tears. Tears. Tears and more tears. For the life you have been given. The life you now get to live. With all of you in it now, and not just a part or a piece of you, but the whole of you. More of you. The heart of you.

This flow is when your heart opens. Even more. That is all.

Everything is always about the heart. We overcomplicate everything with big words and fancy names and fancy things. The mind only takes anyone so far, but the heart is the heart. The heart always takes you back home and then beyond.

If this is your desire.

I honor your path.

For only the brave.

Walk with love.

Walk in love.

Walk as love.

God Bless.

CHAPTER FIVE

Tools Tips Techniques

"Wanting to be someone else is a waste of the person you are."— *Marilyn Monroe*

Meditation

There is a reason everyone talks about meditation the way they do. There are so many scientific reasons why it's helpful, but that's what everyone always talks about. So, I'll talk to you about how it worked for me, pure and simple.

I haven't meditated for a long time. I certainly tried, though. There was a time in my life after that initial experience; I had just recently graduated college and was beginning my life. I still sincerely wanted to know what there was to know for which there was no name. I wanted to go to the very depths of love itself—the depth of everything. I didn't know how, what to do, or where to turn.

Watching a few clips of Eckhart Tolle, Marianne Williamson, and Abraham Hicks on YouTube was great, but at a certain point, which can only take you so far. I wanted to understand this so badly, but I didn't know how to change my situation or life. Let alone the college debt I had to pay off. I couldn't go soul searching like Elizabeth Gilbert in *Eat Pray Love*, Henry David Thoreau in *Walden*, or Christopher McCandless as Jon Krakauer wrote in his book *Into the Wild*. There are those in history who have taken that inward path searching for something, that intangible something, something more, something real, something otherworldly, something one cannot even begin to express or name, something timeless, something priceless, something so true you can never unsee again and that's what I wanted too.

So, I turned to books. It was the only thing that I could think of, and I committed to it.

I read 300+ books in a year. I lost count after time, but that's the minimum ballpark. It might be even more than that because I sometimes finish 2 to 3 books daily. A better estimate may be 500+. I learned that everyone who contributed to humanity has one thing in common. They all meditated. It's hard not to notice that was the common running theme. That and everyone highly believed in what they believed in, to no end. They each believed in the core of their soul; they were meant to do this with their life, and they did it.

Was faith propelling them, something more, or a bit of both? Either way, I always thought that was fascinating and always inspired me. I wondered how a person came to be like that. To have such incredible strength of heart, soul, and character that they would follow this love to the very depths of the world, it seems. Faith is a powerful force that can take us to the ends of the Earth; it's true, for we are always the creator and the finisher of our faith as we walk with love and grace. As many have demonstrated.

Logically, I knew meditation was important. So, at first, I tried meditating every day, but I dropped that quickly over time. Every year or so, or every so often once in a blue moon, I would meditate to find peace when something happened. Half the time, it didn't work, and half the time, it slightly did. During or after my ordeal, I would begin to see how it helped in every situation the slight way it had. It was one more data point.

It would give me a greater understanding and insight into various scenarios, how they are applied, how they alleviate the situation, how they make me calmer, how they relieve the anxiety brimming up to my nose, how they give me breathing room, how I tried to hold on. When you are so stressed out, everyone says to meditate. When you have nothing left, we all try. We pray, and we meditate. I would see the subtle and slight nuances and degrees of understanding of how meditation can assist our lives, but it never stuck. I always took notes! The data points pooled over time as I came to a newer understanding of how it applies and how it applies to my life specifically.

Then, one day, at least 10+ years after the fact, I was going through an extremely tough time where I had nothing left, and all I could think of was to meditate, and I did. I meditated, and suddenly, I went from completely overwhelmed into a wave of complete peace with incredible ease. Everything slowly melted away, and I was washed over with a new sense of calm, strength, and a renewed sense of grace and faith, and my mind went blank. I had accepted my reality entirely, which changed my reality and my version of what I was living. I let go.

I had nothing left, and I let it all go then. It was miraculous yet so normal, the calm that washes over you. To immediately go from a chaotic state into a wave of calm and ease and a blank peace was remarkable. It was, in a sense, like a gentle wake-up call to the present moment. Granted, this was the most unusual outcome and never happened to me. Certainly not like this. I witnessed firsthand the grounding effect and measure on all levels and all fronts. The power of meditation in our daily lives and how it has a play and a pull in the very course and quality of our lives.

Ever since that day, I have never missed a day of meditation. It is only late that I learned this. No matter how much I knew it was good for you, I could never do it before. Now I know. It is necessary. It finally became gut-knowing versus mind-knowing. It's a process for me also, but now I equate it to brushing your teeth. You wouldn't leave the house without brushing your teeth, right? You can't start your day without meditating. It's the same.

Creating that spaciousness before you begin your day is like setting yourself up for the miracles of life. Or, in other words, the miracle that is you. Or, in other words, the miracles of all Heaven and Earth. As you rise from a good night's sleep, sometimes the previous day's thoughts come back to consume your mind, or sometimes it's pretty empty. Either way, meditating helps clear, calm, soothe, and release. It helps you ground.

You are giving your mind a milk bath or a bubble bath, a 5-10-15 minute time out. It's like breathing space to ground yourself. Like any great athlete, you have warmups before any exercise. You don't run a 10k marathon without warming up. You don't do an Olympic sprint without stretching your muscles. Similarly, we do not face the day without giving ourselves this time.

The thing with meditating is we overcomplicate this, too. Many times, we get stuck in our heads about this. Am I doing this right? Am I doing it correctly? Why am I not seeing the result? This is a complete waste of time. What am I doing? I could be solving my problem right now. I didn't complete the full 15-20 minutes, and now I feel like a failure. Did I not do the lotus position right? My nose is itchy. Ten minutes is not enough.

So many thoughts run through your mind as to why not to meditate. Whatever reason your mind produces, saying that it's wrong, we believe it, and it causes more anxiety within ourselves, defeating the whole purpose. Isn't it crazy how we get in our head expecting a result versus just being with it?

Let's be nice to ourselves and not go there. Whatever little thing you can do is fine, and you start there. Everyone has 5 minutes. If by chance you don't, I understand. Nowadays, it seems we have so many things to do with so many responsibilities, all the while with so little time. Who hasn't been there before? I certainly have. So, I feel for you.

What is meditation? Meditation is about being present. Being present means being with yourself. Which means being in your heart. Which means being conscious, aware, and awake. Thus, meditation grows our waking awareness. So, if you have no time, just be present to what is the best you can, which will create the opening for more. That is how people without time can meditate. Just bring yourself to center in all you do and everywhere you go; something will eventually happen for you.

Dipa Ma, a Buddhist Vipassana Master Teacher and a true spiritual master, trained American contemporaries like Jack Kornfield, Sharon Salzberg, and Joseph Goldstein, bringing what they learned to the West. She had a complicated life and found peace through meditation, and said at the end of all her meditation, she learned what meditation is. Meditation is love. That is the truth of the matter.

So, likewise, when we love, that is the purest meditation. It's a purifier in every way and on every level. It is when we genuinely hold and carry and nurture this love within to the best of our human ability that energy, that intention, that desire, if not that heart, that strength, and that courage, is so profound it naturally begins a chain reaction and a healing reaction, that brings on and brings forth and unearths the more, both within and without.

Regarding techniques of meditation, you hear many different stories, opinions, versions, styles, and everything regarding meditation.

We all connect to the divine, our higher self, our heart, the silence, and the stillness or guidance in different ways. We pick up, learn, and process information differently, auditory, visual, and kinesthetic. Naturally, how we connect and meditate, let alone everything else, would be different too. It's more about finding our way that works for us.

So, it's about being open to new modes and ways of meditating and being. Being open to what is—and being compassionate with yourself along the way, which continues to open your heart and keep your mind at bay. Which is a recipe for complete success!

There are many ways to achieve the same goal. Our path is sacred and ours alone. It is unique to you as your thumbprint. How no two are ever the like.

Meditation is essential, vital, and important. Yes, it is true. However we connect is ours alone too.

But let us not forget.

Golden Nugget:

Love is the purest meditation. When we hold onto love the best we humanly can, it keeps us, holds us, tempers us, and releases us. We hold faith; even if we do or do not know what we're doing or what's going on or much of anything, the energy of love is profound. Holding on to that the best we can is also profound, which has a profound impact and lasting implications on our life because it takes a rare individual to genuinely listen to their heart and want to listen to it, and then do it the best they can. Which is, in other words, honoring the self. That means your connection is strong already because it takes a conscious presence to be willing and open to listening to one's heart.

So, Dipa Ma says Meditation is Love.

I say Love is Meditation.

Love is the Purest Meditation there is.

And the fundamental principle of all life, for all time, for all things. It is the be-all and end-all. It simply is like all that is, as you are, in every way that you are, simply as you are.

Prayer

What do we do when we feel alone or frightened? When all seems lost, and things seem so hopeless, no matter what faith we may carry, if at all, we all resort to praying as a final effort in saying,

Father,

Please, hear me now. I don't know if you're up there listening or if any of this is real, but I need help. I need help. Oh, please, Father, I need help. Hear me. Help me at this time. I don't know what to do, and I'm scared, alone, and very afraid. Please. Guide me. Forgive my trespasses as I forgive those who trespass against me, Father. Please. Help me.

Or whatever your prayer may have been. We've all been there. For whom hasn't been lost before and reached that place of hopelessness?

The power of prayer, regardless of one's faith and beliefs, is our path to peace.

How soothing it is when you don't know what to do, who to turn to, where to go, or much of anything, there is always prayer. Prayer soothes and eases all things.

It gives us hope for the future. It gives us a release of our thoughts and feelings. It gives us connection and communion. It gives us so many things one cannot even name or fathom.

Sometimes, I wondered if any of it was heard. Would it be possible? Is anyone up there? What is going on? Is it possible to have all your prayers and dreams come true? And sometimes you stop thinking about it because you have so much going on.

Whatever our faith may be and wherever it may lie or even if not, human is human, and human is divine, and with suitable time, we all make up our minds. That is our individual choice.

Yet regardless of it all.

Prayer is connection. Prayer is union. Prayer is peace. Prayer is heaven. Prayer is heaven-sent. Prayer is the gift you give yourself, just like meditation. Prayer is the release of everything you hold dear, everything you hold near, everything true, meaningful, and everlasting, simply the energy of all your love fulfilled at last.

Prayer is your peace to power.

The power of your heart and soul aligned.

The power of your heart and soul energized.

The power of your heart and soul that begins to shine.

Each prayer is like putting a penny in the piggy bank of love, your bank, and the entire bank.

Over time, it grows and grows, and compounding energy interest takes over. All the math majors know what that's like; growth is boundless and endless. Yet, in this regard, it was the energy of love you offered and gave every moment and every day. The moments you knew what to do. The moments you did not know what to do, and all the moments in between. Even the moments you cried, too: happy tears, sad tears, simply all your tears of love.

Open and surrender always give release.

Prayer is your path to peace.

What is prayer? It's a centering and grounding force. It's where you open your heart and release what's accumulated in there at the time. Which requires presence, focus, and clarity to open, discern, and release. You are processing your emotions, which means you are facing and feeling them, working through them, and releasing them. Facing and feeling anything is always half the battle, if not the entire battle.

As we reflect on life and our journey, weren't there times you didn't want to see it or weren't ready to face it despite what your mind told you? You tried, but did you try? It's okay, whatever it was. Things like this, emotionally opening up to one's deeper emotions, are hard and can be scary sometimes. Prayer lets us release it all if we let it and connect and reconnect to our faith and ourselves, thereby slowly finding a way to rise above the chaos of this day and once again find firm ground to stand within and, hence, without.

Some people pray from their minds, asking God for miracles, money, or something. Still, some pray with their hearts, deeper than the mind, down to their emotions and the nitty-gritty details of our feelings and feeling bodies. To pray with all your heart.

That is what prayer is; a particularly good prayer is when you are present.

And every prayer you give opens your heart.

And that is the power of prayer.

It's the flow and release of love.

That flies like a dove.

And touches the Heavens above. Amen.

Lastly.

Yes, your life is your prayer.

Your life is your art.

Your life is your heart's dream come true.

You are your greatest dream come true.

You are love, true dearest.

Walking

Walking is a pleasure. It's a joy. It's a delight. It gets you out of your home. It gets you on your toes. It gets you into your body. It gets you in nature, the sun, and the gentle breeze.

Walking meditation has been popular across numerous cultures. When we bring our focus to the present in all that we do, such as walking in nature or anything at all, each step is a step that brings you home to now, into your heart, into love.

That means the mere act of walking can be a powerful tool, for it stills the mind also if you are solely present.

Often, we are on autopilot, and something as simple as walking is simply a means to get from point A to point B, from work to home, from school to park, from beach to shower. It's about the goal and not the journey.

Walking meditation, or being present, helps you tune into your senses, body, heart, lungs, emotions, surroundings, smells, physical sensations, movement, and rhythm. Simply the depth of everything that lies ever present, waiting, abiding, both within and without. It opens the heart and brings more mindfulness into your being. Which then, over time, becomes a practice, a way of life, and then becomes your way of life and is integrated into your approach to life.

Through continued practice, you connect, create, and cultivate a deeper inner awareness, an inner dimension, an inner spaciousness that lives and breathes as you do. It is you.

You are peace, goodness, and all the tangible and intangible in this world. Yes, you are that.

As we honor and enjoy this stillness, how we do one thing is how we do everything. So, it becomes a skill, an awareness, a way of being you take with you wherever you go. Work, friends, family, anything, and everything. With greater conscious presence, you can stop mental and emotional hiccups faster, gain internal ground faster, and be less reactive and more initiative-taking in learning the heart of the issue rather than what appears to be. This is how great leaders are born, great souls are born, humanity is reborn, and you birthed a new divinity. For you, honor your light.

Even if you walk not for meditation or even have this in mind but simply for good exercise to be with yourself or because it feels good. Being with self and giving time for self, self-nurturance, and self-enjoyment is powerful, even if it's a simple walk in nature or otherwise.

Through pure enjoyment, stillness, or all the above, one's inner being, no matter the reason we started, naturally goes there and unfolds and lets the story be told.

What story do you ask?

The story of your body, mind, heart, and soul. The story of your work, school, family, and future. The story of humanity and God. The story of all that is and of love itself. It all comes. It all goes. It's the eternal flow.

The eternal flow that comes to you as you sit with what is or be with what is. The real question is, who will give themselves that time? Yet regardless of time, before, during, after, and in between, even all the stories gently hush to a whisper. It melts and mixes into the great beyond until there is only silence. You have arrived at stillness. Everyone talks about this, and you took yourself there, inadvertently or not. The waters here are cool. Just one sip, dab, and swim, and you are hooked for life, and now your eyes sparkle with the sun, for this sun lives in you. You are forever marked with a scent. The scent of your soul. The scent of the whole. The scent of love is everlasting.

The wonderful experience of this life is the wonderful experience of you. Our entire life is for this and this alone. The immense joy of our love. The great embrace of our love. The great release of our love. There are many ways to sink into love, to sink into you.

I used to walk a lot. I still do. This was one of my primary methods to connect, let go, and get into the flow. I didn't realize that's what I was doing. I only knew that I felt better after time. I walked for hours regularly for many years, especially in the beginning. It had such a grounding effect you wanted to do it. It was like a lighter version of going to the movies. It was relaxing, enlivening, and deepening, and at the end of it, I came out refreshed and connected with an open heart and feeling lighter than ever, as if I had gotten off of Cloud 9, if not Cloud 2009.

Yes. Some days, it was really that good. So go out in nature, get lost in the woods, take your dog or cat out for a walk, go to the zoo, and enjoy the quality of your time.

Music/Arts

They say music is the language of the soul and how true it is. Why do we love it so? It captures human emotion; it captures all our feelings and the depth of our feelings that goes beyond words, our mind, anything tangible in and of this world but to the world within, our very being.

Emotions take us back to our heart, and our heart takes us back home to ourselves, each other, and all that is. That is the healing power of music. It has a way to reconnect you and take you to places you wouldn't have been able to reach otherwise. Music lightens, uplifts, and can change the mood and tone, within and without.

Music and all great art can expand our emotional tone and capacity. The greater heights and depths we reach within, the more we can hold, explore, and appreciate. The more we can process fully and clear out. The more we can observe and differentiate the subtle nuances of all the emotional tones and cues that may appear insignificant. Still, in reality, all has a place and plays a part and shows us a greater part and picture of who and where we are at the moment. That gives us clarity. With clarity, greater freedom, and power to choose for ourselves what we will.

Sometimes, when we go through the hardest or best moments of our lives and everything in between, we remember the music and the art associated with that time. Like that breakup song from your first heartache, that movie you cried to during one of the worst moments of your life, or that book or TV show that helped you ease, numb, or soften and release the pain. Music or any art form has a profound healing effect.

Suppose the art, words, or any creation is captured just right, the right emotional tone, mood, or words, in whatever medium it may be in. In that case, it can evoke a healing space and open the heart for more profound inner work to release, like watching a movie, painting, book, song, or just crying. The crying, where you let everything go, everything you held onto that you both did and did not even know.

And in the centering or the releasing experience through the art of any form, we almost come to the ground beneath the ground, the stillness that is all around, because after any release or opening, there is only presence. A true presence like that is always the beginning of everything for the artist and the viewer.

It's similar to listening to Whitney Houston's iconic song, I Will Always Love You. If you YouTube it, when she gets to the high note that she's known for, it's pin drop-dead silent in the audience because for that moment when she is reaching that high note, most people can't get to let alone with such intensity and sheer raw power and passion either vocally emotionally or any which way, the entire audience is emotionally and vibrationally experiencing and feeling the experience and essence of love with Whitney as she feels it and as she expresses it with the fullness and depth of her being.

No one is thinking or over-analyzing. Everyone is purely feeling and being. There is pure stillness within and without for that simple moment, and understandably so. Who would want to miss that? That's why we go to concerts. To feel. To feel higher, deeper, and more than we would otherwise in our daily lives. Then, as the moment passes, the light hum of the audience comes back.

Another example is Hans Zimmer and his music. He is a German film score composer and music producer who has won several Oscars and Grammys. His scores have been in many well-known films, and with good reason. Some even say his music gets you into a flow state. It has the same effect. Any piece that captures that something lulls you into you via your feelings, bypassing one's mind to process the depth of emotion you didn't even know you had or could never touch before.

Lastly, any music or art piece we find soothing, exhilarating, or fun moves our being and gently eases our mind. It doesn't have to be a great masterpiece. Still, we certainly feel that it is, especially if it captured the words and emotions within that we could or could not convey ourselves.

Any great art's power always takes you back to the heart. In your heart, there is a tender stillness and surrender, a presence if you will. Like meditation, if we experience moments of silence or quieting periodically enough in any way, it creates the opening to go deeper, the depth of which is a forever journey and a forever joy.

So, enjoy or create great art that moves your soul!

Trusted Friends

> *"Let us be grateful to the people who make us happy; they are the charming gardeners who make our souls blossom."- Marcel Proust*

Isn't it true? Who can just be present? When on the journey of our being or just in general, when do you ever meet a non-judgmental friend who can be present to listen without any blame or play any games? Simply a place to bear all your troubles, woes, and fears, let alone all the joys. That is a precious gift we give one another to those that do.

Yet, it requires presence first, the ability to be with ourselves, to give it to another. We cannot give what we do not have ourselves. Like love, we cannot give love if we have not cultivated and nurtured it within. Notice I did not say if we have found love. It's not about finding love; you are love, and life is a mirror reflection of your alignment with this love, of who you truly are at your very core.

Speaking with trustworthy friends is a kindness and a release. They create that space where you can be totally and unconditionally you. That is a loyal friend. That is true healing. That is a true blessing.

Sometimes or often on the journey, when one is awakening, or the desire for more has been born within, out of joy or out of pain, usually, no one in our immediate vicinity can match that or even meet that. Sometimes, you may even notice the stark dysfunctional patterns of those around you, but more importantly, our role in meeting those patterns and fulfilling an unconscious need in both self and others. If you notice this, it is the truest blessing despite the pain. So begins a greater calling, a greater desire, a greater yearning for the more in all that means.

What I've noticed, though, even if two people can't find the answers, if one is wholly and completely present to the other, a natural release, healing, and opening takes place, a soothing where one is simply better able to breathe and the tight feeling loosens and opens in our being.

That is always the beginning of higher information, insight, and ideas, along with peace, calm, and answers that come in many surprising shapes and forms, for you invited the lightness of your soul. That is what presence does and is. It opens and releases, and naturally, like must attract like, and begins the healing journey.

From a simple act of kindness, from a simple act of unconditional presence, from a loving, open heart, either from a stranger, a friend, or yourself, no less!

If you have friends you can trust in this manner, consider yourself blessed. If you do not, it's okay; still consider yourself blessed. Wherever we may find ourselves in life, we are all blessed beyond our knowing and comprehension.

God bless the angels in our lives.

Mentors/Professionals

There are mentors, and then there are mentors. Not all mentors are made alike, just like friendships. Everyone is unique, with different life experiences, insights, and abilities. Then, on top of that, everyone has different penchants and proclivities in the direction of their profession or otherwise.

There are many life coaches, personal development coaches, peak performance coaches, guidance counselors, therapists, and various healers around many different modalities, from the scientific to the spiritual. We've all met a few, and I'm sure we have some stories too.

Yet, suppose one is serious about finding peace and delving within or simply trying to understand oneself. In that case, you eventually dive into it all. You dive into every aspect and modality of healing and avail yourself of it all. You see what people have to say and listen with an open heart, see what resonates, and leave the rest.

You never know when something will click, but when it does, it sure does. We are all given different cards in life, and there is no better or worse simply because our mind is our mind, and we all must face for those who choose to do so.

More so, it's about how we use those cards. For each random or not-so-random set, whatever set we may have been given in life, it holds the specific keys to our highest unfolding, the ability to release all there is to release and come into our greatest destiny. To be.

After that event, it harnessed my desire and unquenchable thirst to know. Since I had no one to talk to, no one to lean on, or even ask for support regarding this, simply because things like this don't happen daily, if ever at all. The event is monumental, because of the profound experience and new reality of love it now leaves you in. In all the various texts, occurrences like this are one in a million, if not one in a billion, and are rare, or we'd read about it more often. That and how rare it is to meet those who genuinely enjoy delving into the depths of the meaning of life and love, the true nature of reality, and the heights of ecstasy in their early twenties, if any age at that. For awareness and awakening is irrespective of our physical age but more so our heart's age perhaps, the heart's true desire, and our willingness to be.

So, I only ever had me. Me with all my hopes and dreams, a thousand emotions and one rolling like pounding waves on the shores of my heart and soul that I could no longer ignore. I gave up all I knew and pursued this and this alone. Once you experience something like this, it changes you, so ultimately, you can never go back, for you have seen the beauty of all life, love, heaven itself shining through all things, even yourself. To lose all that. There are no words to express that. The pain was unbearable, but the latter was even more so. So, there could be no other way but so. Of course, there was joy too.

In this time, I prayed for mentors, spiritual mentors, professional mentors; it didn't matter, whoever it was that had the answers I sought. I mean, I prayed for guidance. I prayed for help. I prayed with my whole heart and soul with everything I had. Aside from my prayers as a child during my mysterious illness, it was the sincerest prayer I held and wished for. I didn't want to reinvent the wheel, especially when life is short and precious. I wanted to save time and move forward, learn what I had to learn, and then give it all away. I wanted to give this beauty to the world, the kind of beauty no one has ever seen before, the beauty I felt within my very soul and now danced before my very eyes, the eyes of my heart, and the heart of my eyes.

This prayer was answered years later. I still remember the day we met and the amusing circumstance in which it all came to be, which is a funny story. I had met and would come to meet more professionals with different skills, modalities, approaches, and doctorates in their particular fields of study. Still, none ever came close to the person who forever changed my life.

During our first conversation, my jaw dropped, and I thought, *WOW*! This person was speaking with, and from the level of depth I had experienced and was searching for. There was presence, wisdom, understanding, care, love, and warmth. The experience of this single conversation alone was a dramatic, stark contrast from anyone in my life, back then and even now. Frankly, I was too stupefied to think. All I knew was finally, there was someone, at least one person in this world who understands and someone who can speak to the depth of whatever this is, and from that moment on - I was all in. I was not alone for the first time in a long time.

This person profoundly impacted my life in ways I can't express myself. Let alone, simply being able to speak to someone on matters of such depth and heights of meaning, but more so of such tremendous and utter joy, the very heart of life itself, that alone was the gift. To share one's heart. That was the gift.

We all attract our purest desires into our lives; holding that energy without attachment then it is simply a matter of time.

Anything born from the mind stays in the mind. Anything born from the heart is boundless, endless, and takes you straight back home into love itself. The reality is love is all there is. When we hold love in our hearts earnestly, everything unfolds for our highest and greatest good.

You don't need to do anything; it's already done for you. Through the sheer act of living in itself. That is the grace of what is. The elegant, majestic, magnificent grace of what truly is and how guided humanity is.

Oh, the beauty of all that is. There are simply no words for this.

But yes, back to mentors. I prayed for all the major players, friends, and mentors of every kind to come into my life so I may figure this out and give it every last bit. If you too wish for guidance in this regard or any regard, open your heart and pray or wish upon a star with all your heart. Open your heart and ask and see what arises. If it's a sincere ask, it will be a continual prayer, for it will be a continual yearning. The universe is as it is; you never know what the universe will sing and all the magic it will bring.

The divine works in mysterious ways. We might be inspired to act and go here or there; someone may give you a card, or a flyer may somehow cross your desk. Whatever it is, we don't need to concern or handle knowing how, what, or much of anything. We need only ask then hold our desire lovingly in our being and release. Then, it is done and will unfold into our lives one way or another as long as we remain open.

All is well, all is done, and all is as it should be.

For it all already is.

Amen.

Writing

The act of writing is powerful. Journaling. Keeping a diary and or just getting all your thoughts out. Whatever name you call it. It is what it is- writing out the bones of your being! Sometimes, people get caught in the label of oh, let's journal this way today or oh, let's do it that way in that style in that form. Though there is nothing wrong with that, and there is value in any form, any label can sometimes get you stuck in your mind. No. Let's write out the bones, every last drop.

When I had that moment that forever changed my life, the following days and years were, at times, beyond difficult. To experience the most magical experience of your life that touched upon the nature of the depth of who we are and more and then no one to discuss it with.

That's like going to a Superbowl party, and no one is there. That's like going to the Olympics and no one showing up. That's like going to your favorite concert, and no one came. It's surreal. Let alone the fact that there is no tangible language readily available and accessible to describe and explain this experience, which isolates one even further.

In truth, even with or without that experience, moments like this are what we all universally experience, for who doesn't have moments when our heart speaks to us and we are given the opportunity to choose. The heart pangs and pulls when we know there is something deeper and something true, something tangible that we should listen to. You know, like the calling of your heart and soul and more that comes to you as whispers from the stillness of one's being.

So, I started writing. I wrote out all my emotions, every feeling I ever had. The good, the bad, every thought emotion feeling down to the micro thoughts, emotions, and feelings, and then the space between the feelings. I wrote it all down.

Writing helps you clear your mind, organize your mind, and be better able to comprehend and navigate your mind. It shows you where you are and how you deal with things. It helps you see things in a new light and better process and release it. Then, you'd often learn new things, see patterns and associations, or even grow in the journey of your being that you didn't even see before until it just came out. Our consciousness and unconsciousness are beyond amazing. This is where it all comes out. Of course, I didn't know any of that at the time.

For me, it was just a relief. Relief is sometimes mixed with joy or sadness and every other emotion. Of course, the sheer act of expression and creation was fun, too. I love the artistry of things. It was about getting it out of me; once you express it, you can move on. It was also the only way I could move on.

The sheer act of writing down all your thoughts and feelings without judgment is a form of release.

You go to therapy for release and understanding. You go to trusted advisors or friends for understanding and release. You listen to music, watch a movie, or read a good book to sometimes tune in or out and find a release. You meditate for the benefits, but it's also a release. Likewise, writing is a release.

So, if you ever get stuck, start writing. It doesn't matter what it is or what you say; start. Over time, you will see what there is to see, connect the dots, and smile in glee. It is the way of things. Writing is one way to connect and release.

And over years of writing, somehow it's morphed and taken shape; now it is what it is. Writing became an even deeper dearest joy, love, and passion. It is a true healing on so many levels. Suppose we stay true to whatever path that calls to you. That is all you have to do. Writing was my path.

Personal development didn't cut it. Science didn't cut it. Even parts of spirituality didn't cut it because everyone approached it from the mind. Though still fascinating, I loved learning every minute of it and still enjoy time to time. What I was looking for went beyond the mind. Finding that was extremely rare. That which spoke to the intangible in a real and tried and true way. That's what I wanted. With writing, you are always there. When you're writing from the bones, that's your heart talking.

When you let your heart talk however which way, it's always a good thing, for it is the beginning of the end, and as always, as one door closes, a new one opens. Hence, it is the truest beginning of happily ever after and all your dreams come true. Amen.

Key

Release is Peace.

We want to explore ways to find release in a positive, healthy outlet. Every time you release, there is greater peace. You clear the slate, which creates an opening for the more, for consciousness, for love, for you. You clear the slate for you to arise and awaken within you, giving yourself room to breathe and grow, dance, flower, and show the divine being that you are. You allow yourself to step into the very truth of who you are at your core.

For once you've released it all and continue to do your inner work and release again, what does anyone have left? Nothing. All that's left is everything. Everything that you truly are. That's a lot. That's the journey of a lifetime. The journey of the stars. The journey of love itself.

Namaste.

I honor your journey.

My Way

Was holding onto love.

Praying whenever I could.

Music.

Walking.

Writing.

And later in life.

Mentor.

And much later in life.

Finally, meditation, too.

And the universe has its part, too.

In all our lives, it is true.

Patience and trust.

Is like angel dust.

And all shall be as it is meant to be.

For it all already is.

This I know to be true.

Amen and Namaste.

CHAPTER SIX

Three Immutable Truths

"I took a deep breath and listened to the old brag of my heart. I am, I am, I am."— Sylvia Plath

N ot all learning is created equal.

In our lives, as we do our best to live to what we must, some learnings we learn are quite small but make a world of difference. They are little reminders along our path that add up to improving the overall quality of our lives.

Yet, each learning we learn because we are dealing with it on the level of being or feeling, no matter how big or small, any energy shift is a tremendous shift in energy. It's usually quite impactful because it's a new insight and a new way of being that has just opened within you.

Some learnings are so profound they awaken a deeper awareness and a deeper knowingness within. Some things you can't quite explain, describe, or touch, but every part of your being knows this to be true to the point it awakens your depth. The greater consciousness in all that you do. Whatever name it may be and whatever name we call it, there is a greater self and force with and to all humanity.

Between it all, there are specific lessons and truths to which we always seem to return. Those that fundamentally change or shift the course or nature of our entire being and the way we breathe in our being, for it's about a complete realigning and energetic shift to be here now.

Every great truth always takes you back home.

Back home to your heart, back home to now, back home to you.

Meditate or contemplate on these three; no matter what is going on in your life, you will always find your way back to peace and ground within. If not, go a little deeper, too. Usually, that is the case.

1- EVERYTHING SERVES

2- EVERYTHING IS IN DIVINE TIME

3- EVERYTHING IS IN DIVINE ORDER

Everything Serves

There is always a higher service, purpose, and calling to everything. A higher knowingness, if you will. Once we lock into that, all our troubles and qualms melt away. They dissolve. For it no longer matters. Not any of it.

Not because it wasn't painful, but because you truly begin to see how it served you and the riches of spirit, soul, and fire you gained. While the rest of the world is looking for that something, you have begun to unearth even more with an acute, distinct depth and clarity. Which then always takes you back home, into yourself, your heart, and your higher purpose. The very joy of your life.

That is the power of perspective.

Perspective changes the situation. A higher perspective releases the situation.

It doesn't matter what it is; it serves every event, challenge, and setback. Every high, every low, every joy, and every woe. When you can integrate that into your being, things change, giving you the strength to do what must be done. It gives you the lightness to feel freedom and the fun. It gives you the understanding of how every moment leads to the next, simply steppingstones for greater fulfillment and joy.

Even if one cannot see, sense, and feel the depth of this right away, simply being aware during the moments when we need it the most, if we can remember, helps us to hold on, hold the faith, and hold the light, which is a strength all on its own as well.

In truth, something as deep as this cannot be understood immediately. We do to the point, degree, and depth with each event it applies to. As we live our lives, all these data points of the truth of this seem to merge and coalesce until it begins to take form and take shape within your being and consciousness. Evidence will begin to support this and prove this.

Regardless, one must be open, and the rest always takes care of itself.

Even the most harrowing events, once fully processed, can be the very thing that propels you into you. For there may not have been any force great enough to shake your world enough to change the path you were headed on.

Often, you hear cancer survivors or survivors of a tremendous illness, accident, or challenge say it was the very thing that changed their entire life and even call it a blessing. First, it took a lot of inner work and healing to speak that and mean that and live to that. It takes a tremendous human being to face the greatest challenges in their life.

Sometimes, things happen. Sometimes, things happen unbeknownst to you. Who hasn't been there before? I feel many of us have. Yet, to overcome and bear and endure what you have, and still come out the other side, or even do your best to work through it even now. Only the strong of the strong can do that—only the strong hold onto their light.

Through it all, soul force, fire, and strength are born. Stepping through the fire of your soul, the demons of your soul, and the very challenges of your soul creates a significant cataclysmic shift within and without, and naturally, a new you is born and reborn to the truth of who you are as you claim it and renew it and step into it, day by day, moment to moment, breath by beautiful, loving breath.

This is who you are.

And this is how powerful you are.

At any moment, you can remember who you truly are.

All moments serve no matter what it is, what it may be, or how painful, for there is divine guidance and grace in all things.

May this knowingness bring peace.

Everything is in Divine Time

All your hopes and dreams, who you are, are here for you. When you breathe that in, you no longer take yourself out of yourself. Give yourself the chance to be here now. Where your most significant power lies. From here, everything is inevitable.

When we genuinely open our hearts or do the best we humanly can, everything unfolds simply because we are open to our emotional feelings. The level of depth and sensitivity it takes to be even present in our emotions and feelings is something. Processing them out is another whole other thing. Listening is the key; that is always the first step to anything and everything. For who can be present to themselves?

What is presence? Does it come through meditation? Yes, it can and certainly helps, and that is one path. With heart, nothing but the sincere heart and being present to one's heart, allowing the natural feelings that arise and nurturing the good that speaks within naturally guides us one way or another. Who listens to their heart on that level and degree?

There are different listening abilities for those that listen. It's not so much about the action we take per se, but more so, taking a higher accountability or sensitivity or that listening ability further and holding it onto the level of the heart, of being, of feeling. Deeper than actions and thoughts, but to feelings, and deeper than feelings, the micro feelings that arise that are so subtle but are there.

That is inner work. Feeling and releasing. Piece-mealing it all and releasing it all until you have nothing left - but you. It's a journey for us all.

If we listen to the call within, there is always a natural release, ease, and flow. We become directed in where we want to go, or the path is shown before us. Either way, things show up within or without. It will be that fun and irresistible not to follow it. The opening presented will be as obvious as Dorothy discovering the magical yellow brick road, or the pull will be too curious or delicious or simply plain old-fashioned good to deny.

Like that painting or pottery class you've been putting off for years, telling yourself you don't have time. Or enrolling in night classes to get a degree in fashion or design. Whatever it is, we all have the inkling, the calling, that voice that pulls us toward our desires. When we listen to that deeper calling, that is the depth and the more of you speaking.

A desire doesn't have to be your life's purpose per se, or it doesn't have to have any grand label on it. Even with desires, they are the desires for who you are now with your present state of being and consciousness. As we learn to follow our heart, our heart naturally expands in consciousness, love, and higher knowingness for the simple fact you honored your heart; naturally, your desires will shift to realign to the person you grow into. Constantly evolving, always growing, always becoming. How the joy never ends.

Becoming cannot happen if we do not listen to our heart. The heart is always there, so perhaps it's always happening. It's a matter of time, divine time for all things.

Sometimes, you say you're listening to your heart but can't follow through. Well. That's fine, too, how every moment of our lives serves. No matter what it is. Just because you are not ready now, it's okay. Just because nothing is happening yet, it's okay.

Beyond all these questions, is your heart open? For if it is, you can be present to what is. In the stillness and the silence of your being, that's how we create fundamentally, in our feeling body. Everything is vibrational before it is manifest. Thereby, sitting with our hearts is the very act of creation itself.

Outwardly, it seems like you are doing nothing, but inwardly, you are creating and working with the great universal energy that creates nations, for that is who you truly are. Through the experience of yourself is the discovery of just that.

Yes. Through the stillness of your soul, you discover the whole of all that is and the whole that you are, which only continues to expand deliciously with the passing of precious time.

No one ever thinks of it that way, but it is. Sitting in the heart is the answer to many, if not all, questions, not just the law of attraction visualization for manifestation, which is what the spiritual community is mainly known for. It goes much deeper than all of that. For love is love. You resolve and address many issues simply by sitting in the heart. That is the gateway to everything: all you could ever want, dream, and more.

And lastly.

Everyone has a heart, and who doesn't feel?

We all do. We all have our own time for things.

But eventually, we all succumb to love.

One way or another.

Because who in this world doesn't want to better themselves?

Who in this world doesn't want to feel good?

Who in this world doesn't want to be happy?

We all do.

This is a journey we all embark upon.

That is why everything is inevitable.

For we all have heart.

It's simply a matter of time.

Divine time at that.

And yes, there is divine timing for all things under the sun.

May this knowingness bring peace.

Everything is in Divine Order

Everything has its own time, and everything has its place. It's just not even funny. Really. When you can lean into that knowingness, things change, for you allow grace to come in and do what it does best. Jiggle things. Blow the breath of peace into your heart and your soul.

There is a flow to things. A flow to the great beyond, the universe, all that is. Whatever name you call it. There is a flow to all life itself. The great circle of life, the circle which all comes and goes, and yes, that all flows and flows through and flows from. We, too, are a part of this great flow. For we also have a flow of our own. Rhythm and cycles to our life as we grow and evolve as people on our time here on Earth.

Hmm.

So how can you say there is a divine order when there is so much heartache, heartbreak, and such massive devastation today? Yes. It is true. It breaks all our hearts to endure or witness such travesty, and yet, let's truly look at any of these ongoings. What did any true hardship bring, whether on a small scale or if it was on the level of the world?

It brought communion. It brought back the community. It brought back camaraderie. It brought back the heart on a greater scale and a greater force than ever before, the gravity and impact of which can only be experienced and known by each heart as the fire of love is recognized, reclaimed, and reborn within. It reignited and reinforced what is important.

That is the gift of any crisis. It is a complete and total renewal of spirit. It is the remembrance of love. Understanding on a deeper level the true value and importance of living by the heart and who you truly are. That is why.

It opened our hearts and brought us together. First, it brought us together with ourselves. An open heart means we are sensitive to what is, sensitive to our feelings, and sensitive to be. Be with what? Be with anything. That's what. That's living in the heart. A complete embrace of what is and all that is.

How often we are on autopilot with the day-to-day ongoings we don't even recognize we are, or it becomes so second nature that we don't even realize something is missing. What is missing? Being present. Presence and heart are synonymous. Whenever we are truly present or in the heart, we can be with what is, face what is, work through what is, release what is, and eventually embrace what is.

Through any great tragedy comes the gifts of grace that reveal themselves in loving peace. Keep the faith. It's there. It will come. You will see it because it's always there. When you can lock into it that knowingness or in the least hold it in your being, it strengthens you, reminds you, guides you, and opens you.

Okay.

Then what about all the ongoings of my life? All my dreams and all my wishes for peace. I want to be happy but sometimes fight against my mind. It's hard.

Yes, in truth, who honestly hasn't been there? We all have. So, what is the higher perspective on that? Hmm.

Dreams seed the soil for a new reality. Of course, they do. However, sometimes our dreams feel so far off and out there, if not impossible. Let alone you're right; contending with your mind, too, is quite a herculean feat. It does seem like a heavy ask sometimes, doesn't it? Then, if you genuinely want peace within your heart and soul, honestly and earnestly, that only increases your desire and wanting and calling within. Likewise, you would see the stark contrast of one's reality a bit more at times.

The true beauty is that our greatest moment of power is always in the now, right here and right now, in the here and now. We need not know how things will arise, but if it feels good, inspires you ridiculously, or invigorates your being, then know this is good. That is the energy that will move things. For that is pure desire.

Allow this desire. This is what so many do not do. Once a big or different idea comes in, they immediately scoff and huff at themselves, dismissing it with great dismay to their soul.

That is the beauty also. Even if we did that, living in that contrast of denying self creates an even bigger desire, for the disconnection with self would grow and agitate until you eventually reach some threshold where you are and are ready for more. You are ready - to begin.

Begin to be open to one's emotions and listen to those feelings, and then, when you're ready, take inspired action versus hasty forced action.

So, no matter what happens, it's all happening at the appropriate time, divine time. One cannot speed up time, destiny, or divine decree. Some things are just meant to be. If we just let it. It must follow the natural flow of your life and the greater flow of all that is.

What's more important is to appreciate and enjoy right now. That is the greatest act you can do to give and offer to yourself, others, all humanity, and all divinity. For that is a pure vibrational place to breathe from. Let alone where divine inspiration often takes place, for you are already in pure feeling. When you let your feelings flow, something begins to take shape and take hold. A continual release means creating a space within always to be open. That is presence also.

How everything is simply as it should be. All is well. Everything is okay.

Lastly, it's getting better every day. With every breath. With every joy and jest.

Everything is in divine order.

May this knowingness bring peace.

CHAPTER SEVEN

Closing Notes

"Wherever you go, go with all your heart."—*Confucius*

Y ou are no different from any person you admire and hold in high esteem and admiration. You are no different. For you are that which you seek. Yes.

You are that which you seek, and there is none like you.

When you meet someone in history or life who can stand by their beliefs and their way of being unique and different, may it be, you can't help but admire and respect a person for being who they are. Then, if they have a remarkable passion to follow their beliefs to the very ends of the earth, you know it can be no other way but so, for they followed their beliefs to the ends of their soul.

What happens when you follow anything to the end? You find the pot of gold, a rainbow, and a new beginning. You find the very door you have been searching for, but that door, that elusive door, that magical door, is now. It's here. It's in you. It is you. You are it. It's your love. Yes. Love.

Whenever you choose love, it's the door you create and open for yourself. Do not underestimate the power of love in any manner or any capacity, simply anyway.

For it is the beginning of the end and the beginning all over again. Always.

Every person, known or unknown, who has ever accomplished anything admirable in your eyes, it doesn't matter what it is. Still, if you admire it, that person is like you. They had the same human emotions, conditions, and predicaments. The only difference is how they chose to deal with the pain and the choices they made from it. Of course, how they chose to deal with their love, too, and the choices that naturally came henceforth.

It's that simple. That's it. Nothing else, nothing more, nothing complicated, nothing fancy. Did they not feel too? Did they not hurt, too? Were they not human, too? They even shed tears, just like us, too.

Regardless of it all, they just decided.

They harnessed all that pain but more so, greater so, deeper so, they harnessed all their love. They may have even clung to love itself. To be honest, who hasn't? In the moments when you have nothing and no one. It's all a human being can do to hold on. Through this, they intuitively learned to release their pain one way or another.

Yes, these people chose love and the loving way the best they can and used it to set them free in the manner of their choosing. So can you. There is nothing you can not release into the ethers. All pain can be dissolved if we keep the faith and do our part to keep an open heart; help comes, and as we look for help, too. It's all here, simply everything in many ways and various avenues.

As we let love flow, as its wonderful warm waves whisk and wash up on the shores of our mind, our body, our heart, our soul, our very life, until yes, you too begin to glow, glow with all the love of your soul, which is the love of all heaven and earth magnetized by and through your heart.

Your heart is the gateway to everlasting life and more, so much more. So much more it would take lifetimes to comprehend, unearth, and discover. That is the great blessing, mystery, and wonder called life.

To live by and through your heart, you naturally find you, you naturally discover you, and you naturally come home to the ground of your soul, which only expands as you go. You think you're done, but you're never done. That is the grace, the bliss, and the blessing called life, and our life.

That is one of many miracles in and of this life. Love is a miracle. You are the miracle. Life is a miracle. Whenever you choose the loving way, it is a miracle. Whenever you have a loving thought, it is a miracle. Whenever you breathe, love is a miracle. It is all grace in action, for it is realignment back to self and soul, and is that not profound? It is always profound. The truest miracle is when you remember who you are.

There are people worldwide who are awakening to the truth of who they are, just like you, who want the core of the root of the very heart of life itself. Those who are already there. Then lastly, everyone in between, for we are all on a journey, the never-ending journey of love ever after.

Whether they are known or unknown is irregardless. If the energy is pure, you see and feel it. They are out there, just like you are dearest. We are all simply on our life path. The most distinct and unique path filled with all the lessons meant for our soul to heal, grow, and outgrow all that no longer serves and the yuck and guck we were born with and born into.

Wherever you are on your journey right now, it's okay. You are not alone. Everything is going to be all right. Yes, it is possible. Everything you wish is possible. It's all there for you.

So, if everything is there for you, what about the times when you forget?

If you have been at this for some time or if it has also been your great fascination, questions like this may eventually arise in one's mind.

What else can I do or what can I do to experience oneness?

I've learned all that I can learn: the mechanics of metaphysics, the law of attraction, and meditation. What more do I have to do?

Something along those lines when we try to think our way into being.

Understanding the mechanics and the way of things is always fun. Who doesn't enjoy this for those of us that do? If we are truly open-minded and on the spiritual path, as one may call it, or if we are truly on the inward journey or even simpler, if we are truly on the journey of discovery, it's what we all inevitably dabble with and venture into, how there are so many different modes and modalities, ways, and paths. It is innumerable.

Whenever we are in our love, no matter how big or small it may be, there is an aliveness that's pulsing with life. As we do our inner work, aka face challenges honestly the best we humanly can, then, that presence grows because our awareness grows. Everything expands, even our hearts. It's just our consciousness at the time of being unable to see, process, and understand. It's there, and on a deeper level, you do.

Oneness such as this is with every person. It's only a matter if we lean into our love and choose the loving way, whatever that means for us. That's subjective for us all, for we all have different life and soul lessons. In the heart, do we allow love in or not? That's it, which can be applied to and mean so many different things and scenarios in life, work, self, everything.

The true honoring of self, soul, and love carries with it both the softness and strength of one's being and goes beyond the need to keep or to hold to appearances but to release all appearances. This is the meaning of the freedom to be. For when you are in love, nothing else matters; at the same time, it all matters. That is the dance of the divine, to see the beauty that shines within you and all life itself and to realize there is no separation, for we are one. As a part of this great one, you are. You are. You exquisitely are. As is everything in this life.

You take that next step into eternity by and through your unconditional reverie and reverence for life, your life, and hence all life. Simply, your love. That is the doorway.

You are there. You are already there. We are all already there.

The reality is we are all guided beyond measure only all the time with every breath and every step, especially when we choose the loving way. Then it is over before it has even begun, and you are there thousandfold.

With the energy of love, as we embrace it and allow it, the mechanics take care of themselves. Though still interesting, there is nothing greater than love. For you know, all is as it should, and all has its time when it's time. There is a divine time for all things, and how it all serves. For there is a divine order to all life.

When there is love, everything becomes inevitable.

You are there. You are whole. You are love.

And love is simply walking along the garden of all heaven and earth, enjoying what it means to live and come alive, smelling all the pretty flowers and skipping rocks along the way. Yes. Simply, what a blessed day every day.

So, the true meaning of spirituality is love.

The true nature of spirituality is to give love.

The true joy of spirituality is to be love.

True spirituality is a true coming alive, for it's not what you do; it's who you are. Which means living the life of your dreams on your terms and, most of all, in your heart as the you that you are. Love unleashed.

This is about a true return to love and releasing your love. On every level and every front. Within and without.

Spirituality is often known for one thing or another, ranging from various tactics and techniques about how to manifest this or meditate like that, and yet how rare it is to hear discussions of love and the importance of love.

any from the spiritual and scientific community stress the importance of meditation for many reasons, all of which are true. Yet, beyond all this, let us not forget this crucial principal component at the heart of everything—the reason behind the reason behind the reason of and for it all.

Love is the purest meditation that begins the renewal of all that is. When we open our hearts, it's already there, everything you could want, dream, and more.

It's you.

Yes. This great love you have been searching for is you.

You in your body, mind, heart, and soul, fully awake, fully alive, and entirely whole.

Together with all that is as all that is, is with you now.

Together as one.

To your every joy and ecstasy.

With love,

Jane

Epilogue

Afterword

Dear Esteemed Reader,

First and foremost, I would like to extend my deepest gratitude for choosing and investing your time in my book. The very fact that you resonated with its title and content fills me with immense gratitude and joy. Writing this book was an endeavor of passion, introspection, and a deep yearning to share the insights and wisdom I've garnered on my own journey. My greatest aspiration has always been to provide a beacon of light and guidance for those embarking on the transformative path towards higher consciousness.

I sincerely hope that as you flipped through its pages, you found the encouragement and motivation you sought. Whether it sparked a newfound curiosity, solidified your existing beliefs, or simply served as a companion in moments of contemplation, my wish is that it enriched your life in some meaningful way.

Feedback from readers like you is the lifeblood for authors. It helps us grow, refine our craft, and, more importantly, understand the impact of our words on the hearts and minds of our readers. I would be profoundly honored if you could take a moment to share your thoughts and reflections on Amazon and Goodreads. An honest review not only aids me in my journey as an author but also helps fellow seekers discover the book and potentially benefit from its content. Once again, thank you from the depths of my heart. May your path be illuminated with wisdom, understanding, and the boundless wonders of higher consciousness.

Warmly,

Jane

About the Author

Dr. Jane Yu holds a Doctorate in Pharmacy from the renowned St. John's University. From a young age, she harbored a profound aspiration to become an author and share her vision through artistic creation. This dream crystallized with the publication of her debut book, *Journey of Awakening and Higher Consciousness*. Jane's work is a testament to her three driving passions: eloquent writing, intricate creative expression, and a deep-seated spirituality which is demonstrated in her life and through her blog called *Soul Secrets* where she discusses hope, love, life, and the beauty of it all from our humanity to our divinity to the grace that guides our life. Her endeavors bridge the gap between the empirical and the ethereal, resonating with readers and art aficionados alike.

Connect with Jane

JANE KIM YU

If you desire a deeper understanding, let's chat.

You can contact me at: www.janekimyu.com

Follow me on Social Media

X (formerly Twitter): @janekimyu

Instagram: @janekimyu

YouTube: @janekimyu

Made in United States
Troutdale, OR
02/13/2024

17634340R00136